How To Books

Working in
Sport

D1323706

How To Books are designed to help people achieve their goals. They are for everyone wishing to acquire new skills, develop self-reliance, or change their lives for the better. They are accessible, easy to read and easy to act on. Other titles in the series include:

Applying for a Job
How to sell your skills and experience to a prospective employer

Passing that Interview
Your step-by-step guide to coming out on top

Enhancing your Employability
How to improve your prospects of achieving a fulfilling and rewarding career

Finding a Job with a Future
How to identify and work in growth industries and services

Getting That Job
The complete job finders handbook

Writing a CV that Works
How to develop and use your key marketing tool

The *How To Series* now contains around 200 titles in the following categories:

Business & Management
Computer Basics
General Reference
Jobs & Careers
Living & Working Abroad
Personal Finance
Self-Development
Small Business
Student Handbooks
Successful Writing

For full details, please send to our distributors for a free copy of the latest catalogue:

How To Books
Customer Services Dept.
Plymbridge Distributors Ltd, Estover Road
Plymouth PL6 7PZ, United Kingdom
Tel: 01752 202301   Fax: 01752 202331

Working in

Sport

ONE WEEK LOAN

Renew Books on PHONE-it: 01443 654456

Books are to be returned on or before the last date below

First published in 1999 by
How To Books Ltd., 3 Newtec Place,
Magdalen Road, Oxford OX4 1RE, United Kingdom
Tel: 01865 793806   Fax: 01865 248780
email: info@howtobooks.co.uk
www.howtobooks.co.uk

© Copyright 1999 James Masters

British Library Cataloguing-in-Publication Data
A catalogue record for this book is available from
the British Library

Editing by David Venner
Cover design by Shireen Nathoo Design
Cover image Photo Disc
Cartoons by Mike Flanagan

Produced for How To Books by Deer Park Productions
Typeset by Anneset
Printed and bound by The Cromwell Press, Trowbridge, Wiltshire.

NOTE: The material contained in this book is set out in good
faith for general guidance and no liability can be accepted
for loss or expense incurred as a result of relying in particular
circumstances on statements made in this book. The laws
and regulations are complex and liable to change, and readers
should check the current position with the relevant authorities
before making personal arrangements.

Contents

List of Illustrations

Foreword

I first met the author in the summer of 1990. A long working relationship developed soon after, and James became both a coach and a friend. I have seen him give advice and assistance to countless people who were looking for sports related employment. He has friends working in all four corners of the world.

James has coached me to two World Championship gold medals, a Paralympic gold medal and two World Records; and still finds the time to write. Incredible!

He never ceases to amaze me with his vast knowledge of not only the sporting scene, but that of employment in general.

James has helped numerous people and I think you will find that by reading his book he will help you too.

I am sure that this book will soon become a bible to sportsmen and women looking for employment, whether of a temporary or permanent nature. There has been a gap in the market for a long time for a book like this and I am sure you will find that this one fills the gap superbly.

I only wish that this book had been around to guide me in my career choices when I needed it.

Good luck in whatever venture you choose to pursue, I am sure that by reading this book you will be very well prepared for the exciting new experiences to come.

Ken Churchill
World Champion, Berlin 1994
Atlanta Paralympic Champion 1996
World Champion, Birmingham 1998
and current Disabled Javelin World Record Holder

Preface

Prior to writing this book I have coached or participated in sport in most European Community countries as well as in Bulgaria, Malta, Thailand, and USA. It was also my privilege to have coached a Double World and Paralympic Javelin Champion who is also World Record Holder plus a World Student Games Decathlon Bronze Medallist. I have also coached athletes in sports ranging from basketball to ski-jumping. Further, invaluable experience in a variety of other sports was gained through 20 years of PE teaching.

Many of my protégés sought my advice about gaining employment through their sport and a great number have now successfully fulfilled their ambition. This made me realise that there was little available to provide such advice for these people and that my experience could be of value to a wider audience. Hence this book.

If the knowledge contained in the following chapters had been available years ago I would probably not have gone straight into teaching but would have globetrotted instead. Being a PE teacher might have featured later but I might just as easily have been the proprietor of a ski-hire shop or run my own ski-school. Who knows? One thing is certain. I would not have made my mind up about a life-long career when I was still too immature and inexperienced to make such a major decision without referring to this book.

Numerous books have been written on the subject of acquiring work through sport in Britain and there are also books written about gaining general employment abroad, but not one that deals with the combination of the two. *Working in Sport* is unique in this respect in that it covers the amalgamation of the two in depth. We all know that the nature of employment is changing. It is now very difficult to acquire a 'job for life' and in some areas of the country it is almost impossible to get any kind of work. Indeed, it was recently stated on TV that a quarter of a million people leave school every year with no possibility of a job. To be successful, job applicants nowadays need to be far more flexible and willing to travel outside their area to gain employment. They also need to readjust their approach and not think of employment along traditional lines. With the dramatic growth of the Sport and Leisure industry there are greater than ever opportunities in this area for job seekers.

When I was at school I was advised, upon nearing the date of leaving, that if I wanted a career in sport I should consider the Army or Air Force as I wasn't bright enough to go into teaching, or talented enough to take up sport professionally. Fortunately, school leavers get better advice now but there are still many advisors who are blind to the numerous opportunities available to the sports-minded job seeker. The combination of the EEC employment regulations and the continuing growth of the leisure industry means that there have never been so many opportunities as there are at present to gain employment through your sport. This book contains information vital to sports job seekers looking for a head start, not only in Europe, but in the global marketplace.

Acknowledgements

The following people and organisations have given invaluable assistance in compiling this book. My sincere thanks go to them as without their help this book would lack much of the information it contains.

Bill Adcocks, British Athletics Federation.
Tom Argument and Carolyn Moore at Teesside Tertiary College.
The staff at the British Universities Sports Association.
Tim Burn and the staff at the Armed Forces Careers Office, Middlesbrough.
John Chalice and the Royal Yachting Association.
Rodney Coldron and the National Federation of Anglers.
Jim Eason and Ian Jefferson, Clairville Stadium, Middlesbrough.
Golf Weekly magazine.
John Haddon, Middlesbrough Rugby Club.
Mike Johns, English Table Tennis Association.
Tom Ojasoo, English Volleyball Association.
Lawrie Pearson, Middlesbrough Football Club.
Graham Rayner, Newcastle University.
Rugby World magazine.
Adam Walker, The Lawn Tennis Association.
Paul West, British Cycling Federation.
Colin Wilson, The Motor Sports Association.
And finally, Steven Atkinson, Ken Churchill, Kim Hobbs and Simon Mitchell: athletes extraordinaire.

For the sake of brevity, the book uses the term 'man' or 'he' as being synonymous with 'women' or 'she' unless a distinction is otherwise made. No sexism is intended.

Although every effort has been made to ensure that this book is as accurate and up to date as is possible, no liability can be accepted by the author or publisher. Things change. It is inevitable that during the lifetime of this book some of the data will become inaccurate, and some errors or omissions will become evident. Readers should satisfy themselves as to the book's accuracy before relying on it. No liability can be accepted by the author or publisher for disappointment, loss, negligence or other damage caused by the reliance on the information it contains, nor in the event of bankruptcy, liquidation or cessation of trade of any company, individual or firm.

James Masters

1

Making the Most of your Skills

Everybody dreams about someday being rich and famous. Some people dream about becoming a film star or a successful pop singer. For others the fantasy is of becoming a professional sportsman. Unfortunately a very small number of us actually make it as pop stars or as professional sportspeople.

Every job, in today's climate of high unemployment, attracts numerous applicants, and sport is no different. If you had to stand in a queue of 100 people all applying for the same job you would probably begin to question your chances of success. If that queue was 100,000 deep then you would either be a very confident and extremely skilful person, or completely mad, to even consider the remotest chance of succeeding. The odds against becoming a professional sportsperson really are this steep. They are even worse for women as there are fewer paid players in womens' sport.

Fortunately, though, there are numerous other opportunities, besides being a pro sportsman, to make a career out of your sport. It was estimated by the Central Council for Physical Recreation (CCPR) that nearly half a million people make their living out of sport in Britain. This is in a variety of jobs ranging from coach, physio, pool attendant right through to professional player. So even if you do not have the skills to make it at the top level you could still enjoy your sport in some other capacity.

There are sports related jobs out there for all standards of playing and coaching ability, as well as all levels of academic achievement. If you are determined enough you can get one.

MAKING THE RIGHT MOVE

Would you enjoy it?

Working in sport and enjoying the playing of it are not one and the same. You often have to work long, unsociable hours coaching other people to compete in the sport that you love. Worse still, you could spend all day cleaning and preparing the equipment or playing area for others to use. Would you enjoy it?

Are you ready and qualified for it?

Don't forget that many other people also want to work in sport. Hundreds of applications are regularly received by employers for these jobs, especially in our bigger cities. To increase your chances of success you may need to move away from home or take extra academic qualifications. Are you prepared to do this?

If the answers to any of the above questions are yes, and you have not been put off by the realities of the situation, then read on.

ASSESSING WHETHER THIS MOVE IS RIGHT FOR YOU

1. Examine the flowchart in Figure 1.
2. Find the category in which you would like to find employment.
3. Read the relevant sections in the chapters indicated.

If you are still determined to work in sport, in whatever capacity, it's worth weighing the pros and cons of this option in Figure 2.

Still undeterred? Then the following suggestions will help you in your quest.

IMPROVING YOUR CHANCES

Chapter 6 – 'Ensuring you have the necessary qualifications' will tell you what prospective employers require from you. Many jobs ask for some sort of formal qualification, so, if you don't have the necessary certificates and diplomas, you have three choices:

(a)   Set about acquiring them.

(b)   Look for a job more suited to your ability.

(c)   Still apply, hoping that you have other qualities they might be looking for.

Whatever your level of academic qualifications, you can still improve your chances by acquiring some easily obtained skills and experience, for example:

• Aptitude for car maintenance
• Coaching awards
• Computer literacy
• Council self-help scheme
• DIY ability
• Driving licence

All of these will improve your profile and give you the edge in interviews. If you don't find the more academic qualifications particularly easy, you can still impress prospective employers by gaining some practical qualifications and experience. Community colleges, often based at your local school, run most of these courses and the basic level certificates are within everyone's reach.

Thinking of everything

When applying for a job make sure that you put all of your skills down on the application form. For example, if the job you are applying for is in England it might not seem relevant to tell the employer that you can speak Japanese. However, that company might have a group of Japanese businessmen visiting them during the summer and your ability to communicate with them will give you the edge over other applicants.

An ability to use a computer is always worth mentioning, even if you can do little more than type letters on it. Likewise, if you are skilful at woodwork, metalwork, needlecraft, or other DIY skills, mention them. They could be something that the employer is looking for.

Gaining experience

If you don't have any certificates or skills there *are* other things that impress employers and you mustn't be shy of using them. 'The University of Life' often gives you the *experience* that companies are looking for and many employers place as much importance on this as on the qualifications or certificates you might also have gained.

Simply asking at the local hospital or charity if you could do some voluntary work will often lead to a very impressive inclusion on your CV. Libraries are a good source of information if you need to find out about these. *Yellow Pages* can also be useful. Well over a hundred different addresses and telephone numbers of various charities are contained in most directories. Don't forget that working for somebody is only part of the advantage you gain. Not only do you gain the experience of employment to put on your CV, but also, if you have done well at this job, you should get a valuable reference from your employer.

Being given references

Strictly speaking a reference is written confidentially and sent privately to your prospective employer. If you are personally given a written citation from your employer it is called a testimonial.

However, over the years these terms seem to have been mixed up, so it is worth checking which of the two is required by the company to which you are applying.

The following points regarding references and testimonials should be observed:

- Any references supplied to the employer should be suitable for the job. A reference from your working experience as a plumber might be of little value if you are applying to be a bus driver but it does show your employability, punctuality, reliability and honesty.

- If you haven't had a previous job before then a reference or testimonial from your headteacher or principal, schoolteacher, scout leader, vicar or even a friend could be supplied. They must emphasise the strong points of your character.

- ALL references and testimonials should be typed, on suitably headed paper. Something scribbled on a scrap of paper not only reflects poorly on you, but also could make the employer suspect that it is a forgery.

- ANY references and testimonials are as valuable to you as any academic qualifications. Keep them safe and in good condition. They can be used over and over again.

SELF-ASSESSMENT EXERCISE

1. Is employment in sport right for you? Can you cope with the disadvantages as well as the advantages? Remember it is not a regular 9 to 5 job.

2. Are you fit enough to cope with the workload? Don't forget that it will be physically more demanding than sitting behind a desk, and the hours may be longer.

3. As this type of work is much sought after you may not be able to get a job close to home. Are you prepared to move anywhere in Britain or abroad?

4. Are you resilient enough to deal with awkward and obnoxious people. Don't forget that working in sport is a 'people' thing.

5. Can you work under pressure? You may sometimes be required to work late to finish a project and also work to a tight deadline.

6. Would you prefer to work abroad? Do you know which country you prefer? Do you know anything about the country? Are you prepared to learn the language?

7. Has the work got to be on a long-term contract? Do you mind temporary work?

8. Have you got the necessary experience and qualifications for this job and, if not, are you prepared to get them?

2

Discovering the Opportunities in Britain

PLAYING THE GAME

Ask any group of schoolboys what they want to be when they grow up and the chances are that the majority would reply 'a professional footballer'. And why not? These children would play the game just for the love of it, regardless of the adoration of the fans and the excitement. Money would not be an issue. It is still worth noting though, that Premiership wages last season averaged £4,000 per week with some of the top players getting more than ten times this amount. Furthermore, it has been estimated that these wages are rising at 35% each season. So in their naivety, these boys' fantasies could have pointed the way to a very lucrative career choice. Unfortunately for the vast majority of children their dream is simply that. It is a fantasy because too many people are chasing *too few jobs*.

Football is big business. So big that players are flooding into Britain from every corner of the globe, attracted by the huge wages they can earn here. A good example of this is the Arsenal team that won the Premiership and the FA Cup two seasons ago. They had a French manager with four Frenchmen, two Dutchmen, and one Liberian in the squad. Seven Englishmen completed the total, but as you can see foreigners were in the majority.

This situation is by no means unusual; throughout that season there was a total of 166 foreign players from 40 different countries playing in the English Premiership. It isn't much better in the lower divisions either. Even some of our third division teams are boasting the odd Brazilian and Argentinian. This may be good for the standard of the game, but it leaves fewer jobs to go around for our home grown talent.

It is hardly surprising then that many of our own players are going abroad in search of employment. The majority of those that stay are often relegated to playing in the reserves or in the lower divisions. Nevertheless, a decent living wage can still be earned. Even as a semi-professional in the Northern League some footballers are currently earning £200 a week, and players in the Vauxhall Conference are reputedly earning in excess of £400 per week. At the bottom end though, young apprentices would only pick up approximately £30 per week.

Getting into paid employment in soccer is not easy. A survey estimated that there are more than 2,000 full time professionals and over 1,000 part-timers with 250 youth trainees in the UK at present. This may seem like a high figure but it is absolutely tiny in comparison with the number of applicants rejected. The failure rate in football is very high.

Most players get into the professional ranks by being 'discovered' whilst playing for minor teams. They are then approached by scouts or someone from the management team of a bigger, and often wealthier, club. If they are interested in a player who is still at school, they will then approach the parents or the headteacher. If the player is older, however, he will be approached directly and be invited to attend coaching and training sessions where he can be assessed.

Some players have written to non-Football League clubs and been offered trials, later to be taken on as a semi-professionals, but this is rare.

PLAYING OTHER SPORTS

We must remember, though, that football is not the only professional sport in Britain. Recent figures show that the top UK earners in sport come from motor racing, golf, horse racing, snooker and boxing. Footballers come well down the table. In recent years more traditionally amateur sports have become 'open', resulting in more professional playing opportunities than ever before. The most recent of these are covered below. A list of other professional sports is given in the subsequent section.

Rugby Union
Rugby Union, alongside athletics, is the most recent sport to have gone 'open'. *Rugby World* regularly contains adverts for players and coaches throughout Britain and abroad. The majority of these are for players, but there are still numerous opportunities for coaches and administrators. Most only offer 'expenses' for appointments, but a number of them provide an attractive financial package to successful applicants. There are approximately 500 full-time professionals at top-level rugby clubs. There are fewer than this number in the lower divisions as the less successful clubs cannot afford the high wages and

large squads. Wages obviously vary according to ability and the size of the club, with top players sometimes earning over £100,000 and the lower-paid professionals earning about £15,000 p.a.

Athletics

Few athletes make a living out of their sport. Even the majority competing in the first division of the British League receive little more than hotel and travel expenses for their efforts. Many receive extra money through grants and personal sponsorship but this is still not enough to live on. Money isn't available to pay athletes because their sport does not attract sufficient paying spectators or television coverage to generate income, even for national or international matches.

It is estimated, however, that over 300 British athletes do make a living out of their sport. These consist of performers who are often household names as they appear on television so often. They make their money on the Grand Prix circuit, from television appearances, and from personal sponsorship. National lottery funding is also given to help support the less famous athletes and those who are still developing their talent. The bigger names such as Linford Christie and Daley Thompson have reputedly earned in excess of £1 million over the years.

This sounds like an excellent remuneration until you realise the main season lasts approximately four months followed by a short indoor season. Athletes then have to fund seven months out-of-season training. An athlete also reduces his earning potential if he is injured. He will miss out on Grand Prix and other prize money. However, if the injury is of short duration he should still be able to retain his sponsorship, advertising and training grants income.

TURNING PROFESSIONAL

You have to be an outstanding sportsperson to earn enough money to live well through your sport. The majority of professionals either scrape a meagre existence from their sport or are forced into part-time work and fitting in their training and competitions around this. Some are forced to play as an amateur in order to obtain a regular wage, often from non-sport related employment. Ironically, some sports pay more as an amateur than they do as a lower-level professional.

Most professional sports careers are short with the average being about ten years of full-time employment. As a result, most professional clubs encourage their players to improve their qualifications in order to gain employment when their playing career ends. The semi-professional often has an advantage over his full-time counterpart in this respect because he already has experience of other work and possibly another career to fall back on.

EARNING THROUGH COMPETING

Details of the sports from which you can make enough money to live on would fill a book like this. Listed below are just some of them. If your sport is not included here you can get more information from the national organising body. The more popular of these are listed in Chapter 5.

* Angling
* Athletics
* Badminton
* Basketball
* BMX
* Boxing
* Cricket
* Cycling
* Darts
* Equestrianism
* Golf
* Horse Racing
* Ice Hockey
* Judo
* Karting
* Motor Racing
* Mountain Biking
* Powerboating
* Rally Driving
* Rugby League
* Rugby Union
* Skiing
* Snooker
* Soccer
* Speedway
* Surfing
* Squash
* Swimming
* Table Tennis
* Ten Pin Bowling
* Tennis
* Volleyball
* Water skiing
* Windsurfing

If you would like more specific information about these sports look in the appropriate publications in the Further Reading section.

Remember that not all the sports on this list are wage earning. Some depend on the player either doing well in tournaments, and accumulating prize money, or getting appearance money. Sometimes, of course, this can be boosted by advertising and sponsorship.

Sports like canoeing, where professionals survive merely on sponsorship that either they or their association raises, are not included on the list. It would be unfair to include them as the world of sponsorship can be extremely fickle. Companies often withdraw their funding when the economic climate is not so fair, leaving the participants struggling for an income.

Sponsorship is, however, the backbone of British sports funding. Most sports rely on it to varying degrees to provide for their professional competitors in a way that would otherwise be impossible. There can be no doubt that without it there would be far fewer professional sportspeople. A number of professionals also supplement their earnings by giving demonstrations and holding coaching clinics but if you compete regularly you have limited time to give to such work.

There are several sports at which competitors will find it difficult to earn a living in Britain, but it might be easier to do so in Europe and the rest of the world. Cycling, powerboating, judo, swimming, squash and windsurfing are amongst these. To emphasise this point there are several British volleyball players earning wages with clubs in Belgium, France and Switzerland.

Being a golf professional takes on a different meaning to working in most other sports. If you are making money through playing you are called a tournament player. If you are a golf professional you would probably be employed by a golf club and earn a living by instructing, organising tournaments and running the golf shop. If you are interested in becoming a tournament player then you need to contact the PGA European Tour. You can find the address in Chapter 5.

WOMEN IN SPORT

There are fewer female than male professionals in sport. For example, a few years ago there were only six women snooker professionals as opposed to 626 men, and in horse racing there were 51 women jockeys against more than 300 men.

The prize money given to women in tournaments also tends to be lower because there are often fewer women than men participating and also because there are usually fewer televised female events. Fortunately, things are improving. In 1998 the Wimbledon Lawn Tennis Championships' ladies singles winner received approximately 90% of the prize money given to her male counterpart whereas 25 years ago she would have received only 37.5%.

This situation does, however, vary from sport to sport. In 1992 Laura Davies was the number one golfer on the European Womens' Tour yet she still received less than half the prize money given to men ranked from 71–79 in Europe.

LIVING ON PRIZE MONEY

Relying on prize money is a very risky way of being a professional sportsman as the number of tournaments giving huge amounts of prize money are minimal. There can only be one winner in these competitions, and they attract entries from all over the world so your chance of success is bleak. Add to this the chance that you may be injured, ill or off form at the time of a big tournament, and you will see how risky it is to rely on this way of earning a living. Having said that, prize money is not only given to competition winners. Tournament professionals, for example, can often eke out a living by being 'placed' in tournaments throughout the year.

A good example of the amount of prize money given at a major tournament is the 1998 Lawn Tennis Championships at Wimbledon. The winner of the mens' singles received £435,000 and the womens' singles winner £391,500. Players eliminated in the first round of the competition received £6,530 and £5,060 respectively. Even first round losers in the qualifying tournament, which is held the week before, received £1,035 and £805. The winners of the mens' doubles received £170,030 and the womens' doubles winners £154,160. Players eliminated in the first round of these competitions received £4,020 and £2,920 respectively.

It may appear that a tournament professional could live comfortably by appearing in just two or three tournaments per season, but don't forget that he will have to pay substantial costs for travel, hotels, coaches, managers and agents from this money. These expenses can often be more than £1,000 per week and even if your annual income is calculated in tens of thousands these expenses can still be crippling.

OTHER WAYS OF FINANCING YOUR SPORT

In archery and canoeing the top competitors do not earn money from their sport. The better sportsmen do, however, receive a grant from either the Sports Council or the National Lottery. In archery, for example, a competitor ranked in the world top twenty received a grant of approximately £8,000 in 1998. These top archers can also supplement their income by coaching and giving demonstrations.

TAKING THE PLUNGE

If you are absolutely certain you want to try to make a career out of playing your sport, if would be wise to:

- Know your market.
- Know your own ability.
- Don't aim too high.
- Research.

Knowing your market

Knowledge of your specialist market and its potential earnings is generally gained through experience and by asking around. Many clubs are understandably secretive about their pay structure and their plans to recruit new players. They do not want to upset their playing and non-playing staff or give their opposition the opportunity to trump any of their pay structures, so it might be difficult to obtain information by the direct approach.

However, if you are considering turning professional at your sport you should already be performing at a high level and therefore know many administrators, officials and fellow players within your sport. Buy them a drink and make your enquiries indirectly in a relaxed atmosphere. Eventually, with persistence, you should be able to access the information that you need.

Knowing your own ability

Competitors generally assess their ability in the context of the team they are currently playing with. Obviously if you are only playing Sunday League soccer then there is little chance that any Football League clubs would be interested in you. However, strange things can happen. Even the best team selectors make mistakes, and your situation could be due to one of these.

Several years ago, a Cleveland student failed to make the first eleven of his sixth form college's soccer team. Relatively soon after leaving college he played professionally for Middlesbrough and Manchester United. The student, Gary Pallister, went on to play for England.

Don't aim too high

Occasionally, because of other influences, some prospective professional players can't gauge their ability because they have been out of sport for a period of time. This could have been due to injury, starting a family, ceasing to play when leaving school or a multitude of other reasons. The first step in their rehabilitation is to get fit and then test out their skills before approaching a local club. The golden rule is not to aim too high initially. Start at the bottom and work your way up. During this progression you will be gaining in fitness and in playing ability but also, just as importantly, you'll be acquiring knowledge of the local and national scene.

Research

Before embarking on any venture it is always wise to find out as much as possible about the market that interests you. Acquire a copy of your sport's specialist magazine. Most large libraries carry the most popular of these. Contact the magazines of interest to you and ask if they have any articles covering professionalism and opportunities in your sport. They generally have back copies for sale. You should then contact any clubs or associations mentioned in these articles that you think will be of help. Other useful sources of information are in newspapers and on the Internet. Chapter 4 deals with accessing the Internet.

If you are already playing at a higher level you should know someone who makes a living out of your sport and knows what the terms of employment and conditions are like. If you don't, then ask around. Somebody in your club will no doubt have a contact that could help you. If throughout your enquiries you don't find any opportunities then try to make some for yourself. Place an advertisement in your sport's magazine and on the Internet. Let players and officials of your club, of rival clubs and your regional administrators know that you are looking for employment. You never know what may turn up. Once you have exhausted these avenues try writing to the national organising body of your sport. You can find the addresses of these organisations in Chapter 5.

CASE STUDY

Simon the Seagull contacts the British Ski Federation

In the early 1990s the above method of contacting the relevant national body was used by Simon. He was a maniac skier. He had also been the number one ranked junior decathlete in Britain and seemed the ideal candidate for the crazy pursuit of ski jumping. He had also seen Britain's miserable attempts in this event at the Winter Olympics and was convinced he could do better. So he phoned the British Ski Federation and enquired about the possibilities.

He was in luck. They informed Simon that there was a one-week introductory course being organised in Switzerland that summer. He would have to fund himself for this, but he thought it was worth the expense to get a foothold in the sport.

He mistakenly thought that there was money to be earned in this glamour sport. His first mistake. There was absolutely no money at all in British Ski Jumping. Most of the other teams were well funded by their national federations and were full-time professionals being sponsored by big companies for everything from clothing and cars to hotels. He spent his time at Kandersteg staying at the Scout Centre.

However, during the course the Ski Federation was so impressed with Simon's jumping that they immediately included him in their squad, and wrote a letter to sponsors. Simon stayed on at the Scout Centre for a further four weeks to improve his jumping on the dry slope.

Unfortunately for Simon the anticipated sponsorship was not forthcoming and the Federation could not afford to fund him even at this level for more than four weeks. Although this example ended in disappointment the message is clear that contacting your national organising body can produce opportunities for you.

TAKING THE PLUNGE – CHECKLIST

1. Know your market – understand the type of sport you're hoping to work in.

2. Know your ability – are you good enough to make the grade?

3. Don't aim too high – take your time and use that time constructively.

4. Research – magazines, guides, brochures, newspapers, Internet, etc.

5. Enquire – from team-mates, opponents, coaches, administrators, etc.

6. Advertise – on noticeboards, sports magazines, newspapers, the Internet.

7. Contact – local and national organisers.

COACHING AND INSTRUCTING

You can gain valuable experience coaching and instructing sportspeople without holding a recognised qualification. However, it is very difficult to gain paid employment without one. You are strongly advised to get a national coaching award in your sport as, without it, you might not be able to buy, or qualify for, third party insurance against personal injury or loss. Details on how to become qualified in your sport are contained in Chapter 6 and a list of the organisers of these awards is contained in Chapter 5.

Where is the demand?

The demand for coaches varies both around the UK and abroad but there are opportunities in:

- Sports centres and swimming baths.

- Private sports clubs (soccer, tennis, squash, fitness, etc.)

- Outdoor pursuits centres.

- There is also work available as a local authority Sports Development Officer in some regions.

- Many commercial organisations look for coaches and instructors on their activity holiday courses. Details of companies such as PGL Young Adventure can be found in Useful Addresses.

- Crystal (Adventure for Schools) organises activities in Jersey (kayaking, cycling, water skiing, boogie boarding and trekking) and in Falmouth (sailing), as well as in France and Spain. They recruit their own staff so you are advised to make direct contact with them.

- Travel Class organise activities in Dorset, the Isle of Wight and Somerset.

Brochures for Crystal and Travel Class are not available from travel agents so contact your local PE teacher for information as schools are mailed direct.

CASE STUDY

Lawrie coaches *and* plays for a living

Lawrie is the Football Community Officer with a Premier Division football club. Prior to taking this appointment he played professionally for Hull City, Port Vale, Bristol City and Darlington. He is still competitive, but now on a semi-professional basis for a Northern League club.

Lawrie was very happy as a full-time professional footballer but has never been happier than in his present circumstances. The pressures of playing professional football were intense but now he enjoys more freedom as a semi-professional whilst coaching and working with youngsters.

WORKING IN SPORTS-RELATED EMPLOYMENT

There are numerous jobs connected with sport and, although you might not be involved directly with your own sport, it can be satisfying merely to be associated with it.

For example:

- Community Recreation Officer
- County Development Officer
- Groundsman
- Manager of a Leisure Facility
- Manufacture's Sales Agent
- Outdoor Activities Instructor
- PE Teacher
- Physiotherapist
- Recreation Officer
- Retail Sports Manager/Sales Assistant
- Sports Centre Manager/Assistant
- Sports Development Officer
- Sports Journalist
- Sports Photographer.

The qualifications required to work in these areas are covered in Chapter 6. Once qualified you will find employment opportunities in your own trade journal.

CASE STUDY

Working at a leisure facility

Jim had worked in numerous jobs, including the Health Service, the NAAFI and Quantas, before being employed in the leisure sector. Conversely, Ian had taken employment in sports-related employment upon leaving school, initially working in swimming pools and sports centres. They both now form part of the management team at a large leisure facility/athletics stadium.

Jim's official title is Principal Leisure Manager and Ian is Recreation Officer. They both agree that they prefer their present jobs to anything they've done previously but for different reasons. Ian originally intended to join the Army but he is glad he didn't as he now gets a lot of enjoyment from working with the public. Jim prefers this job because of its variety. The hours are long but the rewards are there. He points out that there are downsides to the job such as dealing with irate customers and the slow bureaucracy. Nevertheless he still enjoys it.

Jim at present is approximately half-way up the career ladder. The salary ranges from about £8,000 for a Leisure Assistant to more than £45,000 as a Director of Leisure.

Ian advises anybody considering this as a career to look in the weekly ILAM bulletins (see Glossary) or local newspapers for jobs. You don't need any qualifications to begin with, but a certificate in First Aid would give you a head start. Once you are employed you would be expected to take such courses as 'Safe Electricity at Work' and 'Handling Aggression and Violence'.

TEACHING

Many schoolchildren are inspired to a career in sport by their own PE teacher. They probably get the impression that the PE teacher's job entails running around playing sport all day with the pupils. In fact, nothing could be further from the truth.

The PE teacher's workload generally consists of:

- Being a form teacher; registering their class then taking them to assembly every morning.

- Dealing with any classwork, homework, discipline and truancy problems.

- Taking lessons in sport, but also taking lessons in another subject.

- Collecting in valuables, dealing with lost kit, dealing with sick notes.

- Filling in assessment forms for all their classes.

- Writing reports for all of their pupils.

- Giving up lunch-times, evenings and weekends, without extra pay, to run school teams.

- Attending staff, department and house meetings.

- Attending parents' evenings.

- Lesson preparation and marking.

- Telephoning for fixtures.

- Administering First Aid.

- Ordering new equipment and maintaining the old.

You can see that a lot of the PE teacher's workload is taken up by doing work that is not directly connected to sport. The most enjoyable part of their job is taking the children for lessons but remember that this is teaching and not actually participating in sport. In fact, a directive sent out by the Department of Education several years ago stated quite categorically that teachers should not join in any contact sports with the children. So the opportunities for PE teachers to play sport and maintain their level of skill and fitness within lesson times is very limited. Nevertheless PE teaching is a very satisfying and rewarding job.

In order to teach you need to have acquired an appropriate teaching qualification at university. This is normally a Bachelor of Education degree or a PGCE for graduates already possessing a degree. Before being accepted at university applicants will need to have passed at least two 'A' levels. PE teachers will also be expected to have achieved a high level of proficiency in at least one sport.

CASE STUDY

Geoff loves teaching but . . .

Before becoming a teacher, Geoff had numerous holiday jobs, including working as a dustman, in a laundry, a steelworks, a chemical laboratory, as a taxi driver and as a barman.

He took a career break after three years in order to travel, but still returned to teaching. He found it far more interesting, demanding and consequently more satisfying than any of his previous jobs.

Geoff's only concern at becoming a PE teacher was that his own standard of performance dropped. When he was at college he was an international trialist at rugby but when he became a PE teacher he put so much effort into the job that his rugby suffered. He would often go to training after a heavy day teaching, followed by after hours training with one of his school's rugby teams. On Saturdays he would go into school early to get the equipment ready, then give out the kit to his own team before welcoming the opposition. Finally he would referee the school game for an hour and a half before going on to his own game. The obvious result was that his own performance suffered.

However, Geoff acknowledges that he would still have become a PE teacher despite all this but he would have made some changes.

He would not have gone straight from school to college, and then straight back into school as a teacher. He would have pursued his own rugby career first, and then perhaps he might have travelled the world.

Eventually, he would have gone into PE teaching because he felt that this was his true vocation. He has been a PE teacher now for more than twenty years and he wouldn't swap it for anything.

THE ARMED FORCES

One of the Army's recent adverts read:

> 'Who encourages you to play sport during working hours? *The Army does*'

This confirms one of the great attractions of a services career to sportspeople. The higher the level that you play your sport the more time you'll get off to pursue it. In other words you are being paid to play sport.

Unfortunately it's not quite as simple as that and there are other demands and responsibilities that come with a services career:

- You have to be able to cope with living in barracks with other recruits.

- You have to be able to cope with the discipline of the Forces.

- You, normally, have to complete your basic training before you qualify for time off to play your sport.

If you join the Navy remember that competing in your sport is difficult if you are on ship. The Army and the RAF are therefore able to provide greater opportunities for sporting achievement as they offer land-based careers.

The RAF also offers the opportunity of enlisting directly as a Physical Training Instructor (PTI). In the other two services you have to enlist for a trade first before applying, and hopefully be selected, as a PTI.

Of course being a PTI isn't absolutely necessary to pursue your sport, sometimes it is better to work in another trade leaving yourself fresh and enthusiastic for your participation.

CASE STUDY

Alvin regrets not joining up earlier

Alvin joined the Army after serving his apprenticeship as a hydraulic and pneumatic fitter. He started this trade straight from school, and couldn't get time off to pursue his sport. Consequently he didn't train or compete again at athletics until he was in the Army aged 23. In 1998 he became captain of the Army Athletics Team.

He is able to get paid time off for his sport and currently trains twice a day on Monday, Tuesday and Thursday, once a day on Wednesday and Friday with a competition every weekend. For major matches he is also allowed time off for travelling and relaxation the day before.

Alvin is now qualified as an Aircraft Technician – Sergeant Class I – and earns approximately £24,000 per annum. He is very happy but points out that he still had to work to achieve success. Like all recruits he had to go through nine weeks' basic training when there was no time off for sport and the discipline was tough. Alvin recalls sitting on the end of his bed in the first week, wondering what he was doing there. Had he made a big mistake? Obviously he had not. His advice is stick it out. It's well worth it. After basic training everything gets much easier. Following technical training you gain your first stripe and from then on things improve dramatically.

Alvin's only regret is that he lost seven years of athletics by not joining up straight from school.

TAKING A YEAR (OR MORE) OUT

The vast majority of students who decide to take a year out generally want to see the world and earn money at the same time. Chapter 3 looks at the different options abroad. However some students prefer to stay in Britain for this study break. Their reasons for doing so vary but some of the main ones are:

- They want to gain experience in industry before embarking on university or college.

- They want to pursue their sport to a higher level without the burden of exams or employment.

- They simply want a short break from working and studying for exams.

- They want to earn some money before going to university.

The case study below typifies this situation.

CASE STUDY

Steve takes time out to aim for England selection

After leaving school Steve had arranged a year's work experience in industry through the 'Year in Industry Scheme' run by Durham University. After this he intended to study at Sheffield University for a degree in Electrical Engineering and Electronics. He had decided on this course of action because:

(a) He wanted a break from the pressures of theory work and exams.

(b) It would help him in future job applications to have this experience behind him.

(c) He wanted to earn some money before becoming an impoverished student.

(d) He wanted to train for athletics.

Steve had one last chance to become an international decathlete at Junior Mens' level. He had been highly placed in the national decathlon rankings the previous season when he was a year younger than most of the athletes above him. This season was his last chance. It was all or nothing.

Now, nine months down the line, Steve reflected on his decision.

He thought that he had made the right decision to take a year out to train for athletics but if he had the time again he would not have taken the same job. He would only have worked part-time as putting in hard effort at a full-time job often left him too tired to train properly. Otherwise he had no regrets, apart from the fact that a severe injury whilst pole vaulting cut short his international prospects.

STUDYING WHILST COACHING AND COMPETING

Gaining a place at a university or college is an ideal way of participating in and improving your sport. The added bonus is that you come out at the end of your course with a qualification and experience that many employers find desirable.

Sports scholarships started, and are still nowadays predominantly available, in the USA. However, other countries have since jumped on the bandwagon and the following sports scholarships and bursaries were recently offered in the UK.

- Aberdeen University – any sport but mainly golf (one year). £1,250.

- Bath University – mainly cricket, rugby, swimming, tennis. Up to £12,000.

- Birmingham University – any sport (one year). Up to £1,000.

- Bristol University – rugby. University meets full cost of living and course fees.

- Brunel University – rugby and other sports (one year). £1,000 to £4,500.

- Coventry University – swimming. £4,000.

- De Montford University – mainly badminton, hockey, netball, rugby and rowing (one year). £1,000 to £2,000.

- Dundee University – golf (one year). £1,000 to £2,000.

- Durham University – rugby (one year). £1,500.

- Edinburgh University – mainly golf (one year). £1,250.

- Exeter University – any sport (one year). £3,000.

- Glasgow University – athletics, golf, hockey (one year). £1,250.

- Heriot-Watt University – any sport (one year). Up to £1,500.

- Leeds University – rugby (both) and tennis (one year). £1,000 to £1,500.

- Loughborough University – any sport (one year). Normally £1,000.

- Newcastle University – mainly golf and rugby (one year). Up to £1,500.

- University of Northumbria – mainly from 12 sports (one year). £1,000.

- St Andrews University – golf (one year). £1,250.

- Stirling University – tennis, golf, rugby, swimming, squash, judo, pentathlon. £1,000 to £3,000.

- University of Strathclyde – golf and any sport (one year). Up to £1,000.

- University of Surrey – rugby, golf and any sport (one year). Up to £15,000.

- Trinity and All Saints College – golf. £1,250.

- University of Ulster – eight sports covered. Up to £2,000.

- University of Wales (UWIC) – tennis and all sports (one year). Up to £1,000.

- Worcester College – paid contract with Worcester County Cricket Club.

Other universities and colleges granting smaller scholarships and bursaries include Brighton, Chester, East Anglia, Glamorgan, Hull, Kent, Lancaster, Leicester, Manchester, Nottingham, Oxford, Queens Belfast, Royal Holloway London, Sheffield, University of Wales (both Swansea and Cardiff), Warwick and the West of England. These scholarships are offered according to the prevailing financial climate in each institution.

Further information can be gained by telephoning the British Universities Sports Association on (0171) 357 8555. Otherwise contact the individual university. Details are in Chapter 5.

CASE STUDY

Kim makes sacrifices for her sport

Kim is in the second year of a BSc (hons) course in physiotherapy at Teesside University. Her tuition is funded by the NHS. She also pole vaults competitively for a local athletics club.

Combining sport and studies has been the downfall of many a student, but Kim manages by prioritising her time and making some sacrifices. She trains for pole vault twice a week with three days of weight training and one day of sprint training. Despite all this she still copes with the coursework of a very demanding academic and physical course. She is currently on work placement in a large General Hospital which is difficult to get to without a car. By her own admission, Kim is only scoring Bs in her assignments which normally would have been A's if she wasn't under so much pressure.

Is it all worth it? When qualified she only starts on £12,000 p.a., but Kim seems to think so. She is driven on when she remembers all the talented people she knows who have blown it all on drinking and clubbing. Kim won't let that happen to her. She sacrifices the normal student life during the week to concentrate on her sport and studies and then lives it up on the weekends. Her only problem is that when she goes to training she is often too tired to produce her best performances. One day things will improve – she hopes!

Coaching opportunities within colleges

The American trend of offering 'graduate assistantships' to coaches wanting to further their education has, to a minor degree, been adopted in Britain. Manchester University and a handful of other universities have offered these in the past. Unfortunately, it is still not as commonplace as in the USA.

If you would like to pursue this option then either enquire about availability through your chosen university or ring the British Universities Sports Association on (0171) 357 8555 for advice. There is more information about this in Chapter 3.

WORKING IN CLOSE PROXIMITY TO YOUR SPORT

Working in a job that keeps you close to your sport, without actually participating, can be a good idea as it maintains your interest and freshness. There are opportunities in leisure centres, hotels, retail outlets, nightclubs, conference centres, cinemas, theatres, theme parks and créches to name but a few.

If you're interested in this option you need to first choose the *area* where you would like to live and then contact the job centre in that area to find out what work is available. If nothing appeals to you there you could then try phoning the local sports clubs. They might be interested in your coaching or playing ability and fix you up with employment as a result. If they suggest you visit them you could use this as an opportunity to check out:

- Noticeboards at the local sports centres
- Noticeboards at youth hostels
- The 'Situations Vacant' section in the local newspaper
- Specialist newspapers like *Jobsearch*.

If all this fails then place your own advertisements in the places listed above plus supermarkets and shops in the area.

VOLUNTARY WORK

Although many people considering voluntary work are interested in working abroad it is possible to pursue this course in Britain. Hospitals and care centres rely on this type of help, and organisations such as Help the Aged and Oxfam often have vacancies for volunteers with many of them covering their expenses.

You will find that this option is covered more extensively in Chapter 3. Although it deals mainly with working abroad, much of the advice is also relevant to Britain. The suggested reading list is particularly important if you're considering this as a way forward.

SELF-ASSESSMENT EXERCISE

1. Which option of utilising your sport most appeals to you?

2. Do you have the required level of skill and qualifications to enable you to utilise your sport?

3. Do you know who to contact to pursue your chosen option?

4. Have you decided which country you want to work in?

5. Can you speak the language?

6. Are you prepared to learn the language?

3

Examining the Different Options Abroad

Many sportspeople decide to work abroad as it aids their skills development as well as their self-development. It can also provide them with an opportunity to travel and enjoy a gap year before entering further or higher education. For some, there will be the added bonus of employment – maybe even the chance of a professional sporting career.

PLAYING AWAY

Making a lot of money out of your chosen sport as a player is not easy. You need to be brilliant at it! You don't, however, need to be *that* good if your aim is just to use your sport as either an opportunity to travel, or as a chance to meet people in another country.

Choosing the right country

If your chosen sport is soccer and you want to play abroad then don't expect to be snapped up if you try European or South American countries – they *will* expect you to be outstanding. But if you tried a club in Asia, Africa or North America, then your chances will be much better.

Alternatively, if your sport is rugby, which few countries in the world play better than Britain then approaching clubs in Europe and South America could be advantageous.

The best course of action is always to be realistic in your aims and it's worth remembering the procedure we introduced in Chapter 2:

- Know your market.
- Know your own ability.
- Don't aim too high.
- Research.

CASE STUDY

Greg tackles the USA

Several years ago Greg spent a most enjoyable time playing rugby in the USA, even though he was only county-level standard in Britain. He also used the trip as an opportunity to tour the country and as a result was given two offers of employment.

The first was to coach soccer at a local sports centre. The other was from the wife of a committee member from his host club, who, upon learning he was a qualified art teacher, offered work as a commercial artist.

A further opportunity, touring the UK with a rival rugby club, arose after being spotted at a weekend tournament, with also a promise of employment upon returning to the USA.

Knowing the market

If Greg had tried to tour New Zealand or Australia, where the game was much better established, he would, without doubt, have achieved scant success.

Conversely, when two New Zealand players contacted a rugby club in the North One division of the national leagues asking for a game, they were snapped up. Like Greg, in their own country they were probably not particularly outstanding as players but here they quickly became valuable members of the first team.

Knowing your ability

This is generally quite easy. If you are playing in the national league in your sport, then there is a fair chance that your level of performance would be welcomed in most clubs around the world.

Things take on a different perspective though if you can't even make the starting line-up of your local league team. The chances are that most countries will already have players of your ability, so your market will be restricted.

As already mentioned in Chapter 2 even the best team selectors make mistakes, and your failure to make the team could be one of these. If you are confident that this has been your experience, and you believe you're a better player than your record suggests, you are still advised to exercise some caution. Don't go to all the expense and upheaval of travelling abroad on a fruitless mission. Test yourself out in Britain by changing clubs. If you achieve more success there then you know that your previous selectors were wrong.

The 'open' revolution

In recent years many sports have either gone 'open' or are in the process of doing so. In other words, sports that were ostensibly amateur now allow their players to earn money from competing.

Two prime examples of these are rugby union and athletics and the opportunities in these sports for quality players and coaches are steadily on the increase. Advertisements for these and many other newly professionalised sports regularly appear in their own specialist magazines.

This is all very well for sports that advertise openly for players but how do you break into those sports that recruit from within the system.

GETTING CONTACTS ABROAD

Researching

Research is absolutely vital. Remember what we covered in Chapter 2 and bear in mind that you use the same methods for seeking opportunities abroad as you would in the UK.

When you contact a magazine ask them if they have published an article covering sport in the country of your choice. Even if clubs in these countries haven't committed money to advertising for players, they are most probably still on the lookout for good talent. Write to any clubs or associations mentioned in the articles.

Sometimes tourist guidebooks and pocket guides about your chosen country contain a section on sport. Use the same approach with these too. Another source of useful information is the newspapers. The Sunday editions are particularly useful with their comprehensive travel sections and even brochures from travel and holiday companies. The Internet, too, carries a wealth of opportunities with employment and sport being just two of them.

Chapter 4 deals with accessing the Internet in more detail.

Finding the openings

A past copy of *Rugby World* contained no less than 17 advertisements for players and coaches both abroad and in the UK. At the same time the Internet showed two colleges in the USA advertising for three young decathletes to join their institution in return for paying their course fees.

Making enquiries
If you are lucky you will know someone who has previously been to a country of interest to you and knows what the playing conditions are like. If you don't, then ask around. Somebody in your club may know a friend of a friend who can help. Finally, if your lines of enquiry dry up, put an advertisement on your club noticeboard, and that of any other club that you visit. Sportsmen are really friendly people. You will most probably be amazed how much assistance you receive – even from players you considered deadly rivals.

Using local expertise
You should already be competing at a *reasonable* level if you are thinking about playing abroad and, through this, you should have some form of contact with regional or national coaches and administrators. Use them. Ask them if they know of any opportunities to play abroad. They, in their years of playing and coaching, have probably made numerous contacts abroad who might be willing to assist you.

The direct method is usually the most productive approach but there are others.

Advertising yourself
If throughout your enquiries you can't find any openings or opportunities then try to create some for yourself.

Place an advertisement in your sport's magazine or on the Internet (see Figure 3). If you are keen to go to a particular region then contact the Tourist Information Office of the area and enquire about placing an advertisement in the local paper. If you can write it in the native language it is likely to get a more positive reaction. If not, ask for assistance from the Tourist Information Office. There's probably someone there to help with the translation. Alternatively ask one of your local modern language teachers to translate.

Advertising in this way was done quite successfully two seasons ago by two South African athletes who contacted *Athletics Weekly*. They quickly became established members of a prominent club in the South of England.

Contacting national organisers
Again, as in Chapter 2, write to the national organising body of your sport. Ask them if they can put you in touch with the national body of the country you would like to visit.

You can find the addresses of these organisations in Chapter 5.

British county-level Basketball Player, 19 years old, 1.94 m tall, fluent in Spanish, is looking to compete for a club in Spain during the coming season.

Assistance with accommodation and employment would be appreciated. If you can help please telephone 01234 567890 or write to PO Box 321, Sportown, England.

Fig. 3. Sample advertisement.

Approaching the embassy

Another option is to write directly to the embassy of your preferred country telling them of your intentions. Ask them about the opportunities that exist and for the addresses of their national associations or any other contacts that they might have.

The majority of embassies are based in London and their addresses can be found by looking through the London telephone directories. Most libraries have copies in their reference section. If you can't find the country that you require there, ask the librarian, they often know other sources. Alternatively you can telephone Directory Enquiries.

Trying pot luck

The least desirable option is to travel to the country of your choice and seek out opportunities whilst you are there.

If you decide to use this method, you must plan carefully and make contingency plans for the homeward journey when your finances reach a critically low level.

Focusing your efforts

Once you arrive at your chosen destination, focus your efforts on the locations that are most likely to yield results. Check out:

- Noticeboards at the local sports centres
- Noticeboards at youth hostels
- Job centres (or their equivalent)
- The 'Situations Vacant' section in the local newspaper
- Specialist newspapers like *Overseas Jobs Express*
- Noticeboards at supermarkets.

If all this fails, place your own advertisements in the places on the above list.

Finally, and probably most enjoyably, find the liveliest bar in town and talk to the locals if you're confident of speaking the language. Many jobs have been arranged in this fashion, over a friendly drink.

Relying on pot luck is the least recommended course of action as it can be time consuming and relies too much on good fortune. It will almost definitely be more expensive than you imagined, and very often depressing through the lack of results.

However, after criticising this method, many people known to the author have used it over the years to pick up good jobs. Several found work in ski resorts, one coaching tennis in Bangkok and another instructing swimming in Hong Kong.

CASE STUDY

Katy excels at basketball in Palm Desert

Katy was a good basketball player. She had recently left sixth form college and was looking for work abroad. She had asked her coach if he knew of any opportunities and just by chance he had recently been talking to a friend of his who coached and refereed basketball in the USA who was looking for an au pair. The contact was duly made and Katy worked for him for six months in Palm Desert. During the day she looked after his two children and in the evening she played for his womens basketball team.

She loved every minute of it but, unfortunately, had to return home when her visa expired. During the following months she recounted numerous stories about her adventure and also showed everyone the trophy that she was awarded as MVP (Most Valuable Player) for her team.

MAKING CONTACTS ABROAD – CHECKLIST

1. Know your market – choose the right country.

2. Know your ability – are you good enough for sport in your chosen country?

3. Don't aim too high – better to work up from the bottom than get no job offers.

4. Research – magazines, guides, the Internet, brochures, newspapers, etc., from your chosen country.

5. Enquire – team-mates, opponents, coaches, administrators, etc.

6. Advertise – on the Internet, noticeboards, foreign and UK magazines and newspapers.

7. Contact – national organisers and embassies.

8. Pot luck – once there, try sports centres, youth hostels, job centres, Situations Vacant, supermarkets and, if you can, local bars.

COACHING AND INSTRUCTING

If you would like to coach abroad then it would be extremely advisable, although not always absolutely necessary, to hold a British coaching award. Many 'beginner' level awards are quite easy to achieve and also quite inexpensive. In fact many sports Level One awards do not require you to take an examination at the end of a course of instruction.

You can find out more about coaching awards in Chapter 6.

Why go to the expense of qualifying?

British coaching awards are generally held in high esteem abroad and are an excellent springboard in your quest for employment. They are well worth the investment. A list of the organisers of these awards is contained in Chapter 5, and there is more information on them in Chapter 6. The same approach for gaining employment as a player can be used, so you might wish to refer to that earlier section in this chapter. In addition, you should also remember that many more coaches than players are now being sought through the Internet. British coaches, more so than players, are usually in demand abroad. This is because many countries prefer to import a coach to develop their own talent rather than bring foreign players into their domestic game. Britain typifies this approach – we often import ice hockey and basketball coaches from North America, but export soccer coaches to them.

Identifying the demand

Good soccer, athletics and rugby coaches are in demand throughout the world, but you need to apply to the less developed countries to gain a coaching appointment in our less successful sports. There are also many commercial organisations actively looking for coaches and instructors to look after sportspeople of all ages on their activity holiday courses.

Details of companies such as PGL Young Adventure and many

others are included in Useful Addresses. These companies are regularly looking for instructors during the summer in:

- Archery
- Canoeing
- Paragliding
- Pony-trekking
- Sailing
- Snorkelling
- Tennis
- Volleyball
- Water skiing
- Windsurfing

and in the winter:

- Ice-skating
- Skiing
- Snowboarding.

There are also limited opportunities for coaches on cruise ships but your duties here may be wider-ranging and include things like running the disco or organising the tombola. There are also opportunities to work in foreign universities by applying for an assistantship. Details of this can be found later in this chapter at the end of 'Studying whilst coaching and competing'.

Taking a temporary job

Some job seekers have an aversion to working for holiday companies as the work is often only temporary or seasonal, yet ironically, it is this field of employment that is showing the biggest worldwide growth. Experts have projected that travel and tourism will be the world's largest employer over the next ten years.

Although much of the work *is* seasonal, many regular workers in this domain make a good career from it by running the two seasons together. This can be achieved by:

(a) Switching their skills from the summer resorts to the winter resorts with the same (or similar) company.
(b) Working a season in their preferred sport in the Northern Hemisphere and then migrate to the Southern Hemisphere to repeat the season there.

Many sportspeople work for the same company for years, often employed in the winter season in the mountains as a ski instructor and then the summer months in the same mountains leading pony-trekking tours.

However, by far the most common way of working throughout the year with the same holiday company is to work the winter season in the mountains and the summer season at the beach. This is particularly the case for many holiday representatives but other specialities also seem to lend themselves to this practice. For example, there seems to be an easy transition between snowboarding in the winter and surfing or windsurfing in the summer.

Switching hemispheres

The alternative to the above is to retain the same sport, but change hemispheres, so that wherever you instruct, you stay in the same season.

Many sportspeople working this method instruct the ski season in Europe during our winter and then transfer to Argentina, New Zealand, Australia, etc to do the same in their winter season when ours has finished. One advantage of working like this is that it offers the possibility of taking a long holiday between seasons as most contracts last for approximately four to six months. Some companies also offer half-season contracts.

CASE STUDY

Peter coaches in Bangkok

When Stan was competing in an international marathon in Phuket, he discovered that the Amateur Athletic Association (AAA) of Thailand was looking for a foreign coach to look after their National Decathlon Squad. On his return to Britain he immediately told his club colleague, Peter, who was a British Athletics Federation Senior Decathlon Coach because he knew he was looking for work abroad.

A few months later, Peter was working in Bangkok coaching twice a day before and after his athletes' working hours, with Sundays off. His food and accommodation were both adequate and comfortable and his rate of pay, although not high, was way above the Thai national average. He enjoyed a decent quality of life and he had plenty of time for sightseeing and relaxing.

Peter enjoyed the work and the Thai athletes and administrators seemed to like him also. They wanted him to work there for a year but due to business commitments in the UK he had to decline and negotiated a three-month contract.

It is several years since Peter was in Bangkok, but the Secretary of their AAA invites him back to coach every year. Maybe, if he can put his commitments in the UK on hold, he will return to coach again one day. He would certainly love to.

Fig. 4. Examples of the sort of job advertisements you might see
in magazines.

VOLUNTARY WORK

Many people have a misconception about voluntary work abroad because it suggests that you are working for no salary. Yet, in the majority of cases, this is simply not true. Remuneration varies greatly, from those organisations who provide nothing but food and accommodation to others who provide these plus a wage. In general, the vast majority of agencies simply provide pocket money on top of basic accommodation and food. However, there are some that pay a higher wage than many travel and leisure companies. Take care in your selection. A few agencies charge a registration fee, and surprisingly, offer much lower remuneration.

Before volunteering make sure you are clear about how long you want to spend in this type of work as periods of employment can range from one week to three years.

There are several books in the Further Reading section that go into greater detail if you are interested in pursuing this option.

Illustrating recent opportunities

There have recently, through Voluntary Service Overseas (VSO), been opportunities to work in sport in Africa, Asia and Eastern Europe. These positions were mainly in the Sports Development Officer domain so coaching, teaching and management experience would be required. The appointments were for two years and you needed to be at least 20 years old.

VSO are a well established and respected organisation, and they do their utmost to cater for all of their volunteers' requirements. All travel arrangements are organised and paid for by them. Before leaving Britain volunteers recently received approximately £500 to buy suitable clothing and equipment and another £250 half-way through their contract. A salary is paid at the local rate and, although being nowhere near UK levels, it is more than adequate to live on in that country. Accommodation and medical insurance is also provided.

There are a number of advantages to volunteering:

- Knowing that you are doing a job that is really worthwhile.

- All the arrangements are made for you.

- Working in a team with definite objectives.

- You will have the chance to see the problems and the sights of a third world country at first hand.

- Voluntary work always looks impressive on a CV when applying for jobs on return to the UK.

CASE STUDY

John finds fulfilment in Belize

John was 25 and a teacher in an inner city school. He felt that he was getting nowhere in his job. He had worked at the same school since leaving university but had tried to leave several times. His applications for appointments in other schools achieved no success and he felt trapped. His pay was poor and his morale very low. He wanted to do a job that was more rewarding, not necessarily financially, but one where he felt that he was achieving something.

John applied to Voluntary Service Overseas and he was invited to attend an assessment day in Manchester. He was then trained and briefed in Birmingham and, barely before he had time to think, he found himself in Belize teaching woodwork in a technical college and enjoyed it so much that he extended his two-year contract to four.

John is now back at home in Sheffield enjoying a well earned break while he considers his future. He is quite attracted to VSO work again, but maybe this time in a different country so he can experience a different culture.

CAMP COUNSELLING AND SUMMER CAMPS

The idea of summer camps started in the USA and North America is still the major destination for sports enthusiasts pursuing this option, although several holiday companies now have their own in many countries around the world.

The biggest names in summer camps are still BUNAC and Camp America. Between them they offer sports-related work in:

• Aerobics	• Diving	• Karate	• Soccer
• Archery	• Fencing	• Lacrosse	• Swimming
• Athletics	• Golf	• Life-saving	• Tennis
• Baseball	• Gymnastics	• Motorboating	• Volleyball
• Basketball	• Hiking	• Rifle-shooting	• Water-skiing
• Camping†	• Hockey	• Rock-climbing	• Weight-training
• Canoeing*	• Horseriding	• Roller-blading	• Windsurfing
• Cycling	• Judo	• Sailing	

†offers other specialisms of outdoor cooking, campcraft and ropes course
*offers other specialisms of kayaking and canoeing expeditions.

To help you with your decision-making, a list of what both Camp America and BUNAC offer is included here. More information is available from each organisation (see Useful Addresses).

• Orientation training before commencing work.

• Arranging work papers and visas.

• Return air fare, and transfers to and from your camp.

• Food and accommodation.

• A salary.

• Six or seven weeks' holiday time after camp before returning to your home country.

BUNAC

BUNAC stands for British Universities North America Club, and they arrange employment at summer camps in the USA and Canada. They have become so well established since their inauguration in 1962 that they now arrange work in many other countries. Some of their employment is also of the non-sporting type, this programme currently includes opportunities in Australia, Ghana, Jamaica, Malta, New Zealand, Spain and South Africa.

There is a registration fee (refundable if unsuccessful) and a membership fee if you obtain work through BUNAC. In addition, you will have to pay for:

(a) Travel to your interview, and orientation, at a university close to you.

(b) Your own medical.

(c) Your own visa.

(d) Medical, accident and baggage insurance.

Rates of pay vary and you are advised to establish your remuneration before you take up the appointment with BUNAC (see Useful Addresses).

Camp America

Camp America have been running summer camps for 29 years. They don't organise work outside of the USA but they do offer a wider range of sporting activities. Interviews are held all over the UK so, if you reach that stage, you will not have too far to travel. You will not be required to undergo a medical examination but you will have to complete a medical form. If you are given a placement you will need to get confirmation of your medical history from your doctor who will also have to confirm your suitability for the programme. These costs are met by you. At your interview you will have to pay a first deposit followed by a second payment if you obtain a placement. This, however, includes your visa fee and airport taxes.

The amount you will be paid depends on your age, type of job, and experience. Details are available from the organisation (see Useful Addresses).

Looking at other camps around the world

Following the American example, summer camps and activity holidays have become popular in many other countries and the majority of these are organised for children. Brochures are not easy to come by but, as the majority of companies specialising in these holidays mail direct to schools, ask your local PE teacher if they have any spare copies and take your contact addresses from these. Alternatively, you can sometimes find advertisements for these holidays in national newspapers.

Although travel agents don't stock large numbers of these brochures it's still worth checking them out.

CASE STUDY

Karen visits the Grand Canyon, courtesy of BUNAC

Karen got the idea for working in summer camps from friends at college. She was in her second year of teacher training when she applied to BUNAC.

After being accepted she flew out to Kenwood Camp in Connecticut, where she was employed to coach tennis. She enjoyed it so much that she returned to the same camp the following year, this time as a group leader, looking after 22 eleven-year-olds.

Karen said that if her circumstances were different she would have done the same thing again this summer but family commitments prevented her from doing so.

She confessed that 'Working with BUNAC has been an important part of my life. I really enjoyed the work. It also assisted in financing my tour of the States as I could not have afforded to see the Grand Canyon and other sights in America without it. I am positive that having this on my CV also helped me to secure my current teaching post.'

TAKING A YEAR (OR MORE) OUT

If past experiences are borne out, many people reading this book will be school leavers or university graduates who want to see a bit more of the world before settling down to the next phase of their career.

This is not a bad idea. Many people, including future employers, think that a break from the education system not only helps you to apply yourself to future studies but also that you will be a more mature, capable person as a result of your travels and experiences.

Sometimes taking a year out can change your career plan and you might decide against going back to college in the immediate future. All the options listed in this book are ideal ways for you to gain employment. The seasonal and voluntary work sections should be particularly pertinent. However, if you are still debating this option and would like more information on the matter there are several books on the subject listed in the Further Reading section. These are normally stocked by your local library.

CASE STUDY

Tracy decides on an extension to her work experience

Tracy was fairly typical of most school leavers. She was intelligent enough to get good passes in several GCSEs and was advised to go on to study at college where she enrolled on a Leisure and Tourism course. Part of her studies required her to spend eight weeks on work experience in a French ski resort. She enjoyed it so much she never returned.

Tracy worked her first year as a chambermaid before applying for a job with the same company as a skiing representative. Her qualifications and college work in the travel industry were big assets in gaining this position. She has done this work for three seasons now but thinks that she will do something else soon. Exactly what she will do is still undecided but her experience gives her a wide range of options.

STUDYING WHILST COACHING AND COMPETING

Sports scholarships started, and are still predominantly available, in the USA.

Historically much of the USA's sporting success was college based, and even today college sport plays a major role in the sporting achievements of that nation.

Although there are limited opportunities to win sports scholarships in universities and colleges worldwide, the vast majority of such opportunities are still in America. Students here can only be signed to a college sports team between 15 April and 1 August to comply with their strict National Collegiate Athletic Association (NCAA) rules.

Getting a sports scholarship at a university or college has two major advantages:

(a) It is a great way of playing and improving your sport.

(b) If you work hard enough you finish your course with a qualification and experience that many employers find desirable.

Coaching opportunities

If your forte is coaching you could work your way through the system by applying for a postgraduate 'assistantship' at a college or university. As the title suggests, you would apply to work as an assistant coach for one of the college sports teams and, in return, you receive your postgraduate tuition and accommodation free of charge. This not only enables you to come out with a higher-level degree, but also gives you valuable contacts within the system which may eventually lead to further opportunities.

Most of these assistantship opportunities exist in American universities but there have been some in British institutions in recent years. Normally, if you want to pursue this option, you should contact your chosen university yourself. However, some universities occasionally advertise such opportunities on the Internet.

Avoiding the pitfalls

If these opportunities look enticing and desirable you should heed a few words of warning. Whilst the vast majority of students returning to the UK after completing an assisted course recount their great times, there have also been a small number of horror stories. Some students have returned, often without completing their course, because of the excessive pressure they were under from the college's

Head Coach. They have complained about such things as being asked to compete whilst still injured, or to take on different roles within their sport than they are used to. For example – going there as a high jumper and being asked also to fill in as a javelin thrower and relay runner to gain valuable points for their college team. Non-compliance with the coach's requests is often then followed by the threat of withdrawal of the students funding.

This is a case of 'he who pays the fiddler calls the tune' and can be understandable when the coach is under enormous pressure to produce results. However it must be pointed out that this is not the norm. The majority of coaches conduct themselves in a totally professional manner.

The best way to avoid this happening is to extensively research your preferred college. Also, if finances permit, visit it and talk to the coaching staff and students. Remember though that the higher the level that you compete at, the more valuable you are to them, so there is less likelihood of being used as a dogsbody.

To research the opportunities available, read *Sports Scholarships and College Programs in the USA*. This is an absolutely invaluable book and full details are in the bibliography. It comprehensively covers all aspects of sports scholarships in the USA.

CASE STUDY

James competes for Maryland

James competed as a decathlete for Great Britain at the World Junior Championships whilst at sixth form college. When it was time to apply for university he sensibly talked over his options with his coach and the Great Britain Team Manager. The latter recommended a college in the USA that was keen to attract decathletes and also had a good academic reputation. Consequently James enrolled, enjoyed his studies, graduated and began working as a teacher in Maryland whilst also competing for them. Unfortunately his work permit expired and he had to return home for a short period.

He overcame this problem by applying, and being accepted, to do a masters degree at a different US university. He is at present halfway through the first year of this course, whilst also enjoying his sport.

WORKING IN SPORTS-RELATED EMPLOYMENT

There are numerous jobs closely connected with sport that could also give rise to employment abroad. They might not involve you directly with your own sport but the work may be satisfying merely through being associated with it. The list of British jobs contained in Chapter 2 is obviously relevant to other countries but it does have some exceptions. For example, some of the third world countries may not be wealthy enough to employ county development officers.

Opportunities for employment in sports-related jobs exist globally but employers would expect you to have experience in your own country before seeking work abroad. If you want to investigate this option further then refer to Chapters 2 and 6 to help you assess the market and identify the qualifications you will need. Once qualified you can start applying for opportunities advertised in your own sport journal.

WORKING IN CLOSE PROXIMITY TO YOUR SPORT

If you would like to work in a job that keeps you in close proximity to your sport, without actually participating – for example working in a ski resort in a domestic capacity and using your leisure time to ski – then there are countless opportunities for employment.

Leisure is one of the few worldwide growth industries. Experts estimate that the travel industry in Britain is growing at two and a half times that of gross national product.

Many leisure companies employ thousands of employees both in Britain and abroad and the Internet regularly contains advertisements from leisure companies in Canada and the USA for positions in national parks, ski resorts, cruise ships, river jobs, camp jobs, ranch jobs and volunteering.

Finding the right job for yourself

Holiday companies in particular require people to work as:

- Accounts clerk
- Administrative assistant
- Airport executive
- Babysitter
- Bar staff
- Beautician
- Boiler technician
- Boat maintenance
- Bus driver/staff
- Campsite courier
- Campsite services attendant
- Carpenter
- Centre manager
- Chalet maid
- Chambermaid
- Coffee bar staff
- Cook/kitchen attendant
- Courier
- Croupier
- Dishwasher

- Driver
- Electrician
- Entertainer
- Entertainment organiser
- Fibre-glasser
- Fire-safety officer
- Groundsman
- Group leader
- Hairdresser
- Handyman
- Holiday representative
- Instructor
- Interpreter
- Janitor
- Kindergarten teacher
- Holiday representative
- Manager
- Mechanic
- Musician
- Nanny
- Night auditor
- Nurse
- Office staff
- Painter
- Photographer
- Plumber
- Porter
- Printer
- Receptionist
- Rescue-boat personnel
- Rodent control officer
- Service station staff
- Sewing machinist
- Shipping clerk
- Shop worker
- Ski technician
- Ski-lift attendant
- Ski-lift mechanic
- Store assistant
- Teacher
- Telephone operator
- Ticket collector
- Tour guide
- Waiter/waitress.

Working in the leisure industry

If you want to pursue this option make sure you apply at the right time. Most leisure companies start recruiting for their winter season between April and August but there can still be some vacancies available in the Autumn. Companies requiring summer workers generally accept applications between the previous September and February but, again, last minute applicants have been successful as late as April. Obviously in all cases the earlier you apply the more choice you have and the greater your chance of success.

If you don't necessarily want to work in a job connected with your sport, but merely obtain employment close to the facilities that you need, then the opportunities are endless. Many newspapers and magazines carry advertisements from employers abroad asking British men and women to work for them. *The Lady*, for example, carries multitude of opportunities for women to work as nannies abroad.

This can be a good way to earn some money and enjoy your sport, because this option has several advantages over other kinds of work:

- You are still fresh and keen for your sport when you have finished your daily job.

- You are probably close to your sport's 'arena'.

- You are surrounded by like-minded people.

In other lines of sports-related work many people become disillusioned when they realise they have no time or energy to participate having spent all day coaching/teaching it.

You can find some examples of past opportunities under 'Work not directly connected to your sport' in Chapter 4 and more ideas can be formulated from the list of journals in Useful Addresses or Further Reading.

CASE STUDY

Bernadette needed a career break

Bernadette had achieved everything that she had aimed for by the time she was 25. She had worked in banking since leaving school and she now owned her own house and a car. Although she was very comfortable she was unsettled and felt she needed a career break.

At the time of being interviewed Bernadette was working as a chambermaid at the Les Orres ski resort in France. She was happy with the work as it was not too demanding and gave her a chance to take part in her sport but, again, she was in reflective mood.

She was using her career break to decide:

(a) Whether to say with this company and try to work her way up into management.

(b) Whether to go back to college and take a postgraduate course in education to qualify as a teacher.

THE ARMED FORCES

As with Britain, opportunities exist to pursue your sport whilst working in the Armed Forces of a foreign country. It is extremely rare for a British national to do this, but there are cases of sportsmen doing so. Steve Tunstall, for example, was a GB cross country international who served his time in the French Foreign Legion.

If you are interested in pursuing this as an idea then you should contact the appropriate embassy. The majority of these are listed in the London telephone directory which can be found in most main libraries.

SELF-ASSESSMENT EXERCISE

1. Which option for using your sport most appeals to you?

2. Do you have the required level of skill and qualifications to enable you to utilise your sport?

3. Do you know who to contact to pursue your chosen option?

4. Have you decided which country you want to work in?

5. Can you speak the language?

6. Are you prepared to learn the language?

4

Finding Employment

ACCESSING THE INFORMATION

Employment opportunities in sport can be found advertised in sports centres, job centres, sports clubs, books, magazines, newspapers and on the Internet as well as numerous other venues. There are also many privately owned employment agencies that can arrange a job for you. For example – a company called Career Search, which specialises in sports-related recruitment, advertises on the Internet. Most of these private companies, however, charge a fee so check out all the free opportunities first. It goes without saying that if you don't read a national sports magazine, or don't have access to the Internet, then you are reducing your range of opportunities.

If you can afford it you should subscribe to them both but you can take advantage of these sources in other ways. Ask around your sports club for someone you can borrow the magazines from. If that's a non-starter, note that some of the bigger libraries stock the most popular sports magazines in their reference section. A list of many of these journals is included in the Further Reading section.

Accessing the Internet

The cheapest way to access the Internet is to ask your friends if any of them are on line or visit your local school or college and ask if you can use their facilities.

Accessing the Internet is now much easier with computer bureaux being established around the country. Many of them sited in central libraries. The fees for using them are very reasonable with some operators charging nothing for the first half-hour and then a nominal fee for every half-hour after that. They often also give instruction free of charge.

There are also commercial organisations such as the Internet Cafés or the Cyber Cafés where a small fee gives access to their facilities. Look in *Yellow Pages* and don't forget to enquire about their charges.

If you are unsure about how to use the Internet, or indeed what it is, there are numerous books on the subject stocked by all major libraries.

FINDING YOUR SPORT

The following list contains opportunities that have been recently advertised in company literature, books, magazines, newspapers, job centres or on the Internet. You can find the full addresses, telephone, fax numbers and Internet details in Useful Addresses. It is by no means a complete list and the intention is merely to give you an example of the range of possibilities usually available in this type of work. Although much of the work is seasonal it is often available every year and many sportspeople return to work for the same company year after year.

For each opportunity listed, a reference is given to enable you to get more specific details from Useful Addresses. The jobs require differing levels of qualifications so please check before applying for anything by contacting the person or department named against your chosen company.

In each category the sport is given in bold type, with employers' names listed alphabetically below this. The location(s) in which they operate follows and, finally, a Useful Addresses reference. Work in Britain is given at the start of each category.

JOBS THAT ARE USUALLY AVAILABLE

Key: Bk. = Book.   Co. = Company   literature/references.   Int. = Internet. Mag. = Magazine. News. = Newspaper.

Aerobics and Fitness

PGL Young Adventure.	Britain, France & Spain.	Co.
Colossus Beach Hotel.	Greece.	Bk.
Just Cruising International.	Caribbean.	Int.
Mark Warner.	Corsica, Italy, Sardinia, Greece & Turkey.	Co.
Camden County YMCA.	USA.	Int.

American Football

PGL Young Adventure.	Britain, France & Spain.	Co.
University of Hawaii.	USA.	Int.

Angling and Fishing

PGL Young Adventure.	Britain, France & Spain.	Co.
Home Ranch.	USA.	Int.
Great Alaska Fish Camp.	USA.	Int.
Vista Verde Ranch.	USA.	Int.

Archery

PGL Young Adventure.	Britain, France & Spain.	Co.
West of Ireland Activity Centre.	Ireland.	Bk.
Club Mediterranee.	Europe & North Africa.	Bk.

Athletics – Track and Field and Cross County

Cleveland State University.	USA.	Int.
University of Idaho.	USA.	Int.
University of North Carolina.	USA.	Int.

Badminton

PGL Young Adventure.	Britain, France & Spain.	Co.

Basketball

PGL Young Adventure.	Britain, France & Spain.	Co.
University of Southern California.	USA.	Int.

Camping

PGL Young Adventure.	Britain, France & Spain.	Co.
Backroads.	USA & Mexico.	Co.
Canvas Holidays.	Throughout Europe.	Co.
Eurocamp.	Throughout Europe.	Co.
Keycamp Holidays.	Throughout Europe.	Co.
Suntrek Tours.	USA & Mexico.	Int.
Great Alaska Fish Camp.	USA.	Int.

Canoeing, Kayaking and Rafting

Crystal Schools.	France & Jersey.	Co.
PGL Young Adventure.	Britain, France & Spain.	Co.
West of Ireland Activity Centre.	Ireland.	Bk.
Backroads.	Canada.	Co.
Camp Duncan.	USA.	Int.
Canvas Holidays.	Throughout Europe.	Co.
Headwater Holidays.	France.	Co.

Caving

PGL Young Adventure.	Britain, France & Spain.	Co.

Cricket

PGL Young Adventure.	Britain, France & Spain.	Co.

Cycling and Mountain Biking

PGL Young Adventure.	Britain, France & Spain.	Co.
Backroads.	Worldwide.	Int.
Belle France.	France.	Bk.

Diving – Scuba and Snorkelling

Backroads.	New Mexico.	Co.
Club Mediterranee.	Europe & North Africa.	Co.
Rotfluhhotel.	Austria.	Bk.
Emperor Divers.	Egypt.	Bk.

Equestrianism

Arundel Farm.	New Zealand.	Int.
PGL Young Adventure.	Britain, France & Spain.	Co.
Errislannan Manor.	Ireland.	Bk.
High Meadow Ranch.	USA.	Int.

Fencing

PGL Young Adventure.	Britain, France & Spain.	Co.

General

There are numerous opportunities here and you should refer to the section on 'Work not directly connected to your Sport' on page 69.

Golf

Came Down Golf Club.	Britain.	Mag.
Drayton Park Golf Club.	Britain.	Mag.
Hever Golf Club.	Britain.	Mag.
Jack Nicklaus Golf Centre.	Britain.	Mag.
La Moye Golf Club.	Jersey.	Mag.
Lamberhurst Golf Club.	Britain.	Mag.
The London Golf Club.	Britain.	Mag.
Royal Ashdown Forest Golf Club.	Britain.	Mag.
Tandridge Golf Club.	Britain.	Mag
Three Rivers Golf Club.	Britain.	Mag
Club Mediterranee.	Europe & North Africa.	Co.
Golf Centrum.	Rotterdam.	Mag.

Hockey

PGL Young Adventure.	Britain, France & Spain.	Co.

Ice Hockey

University of Maine.	USA.	Int.

Lacrosse

T. Jefferson High School.	USA.	Int.

Mini Motorsports and Karting

PGL Young Adventure.	Britain, France & Spain.	Co.
Camp America.	USA.	Co.

Netball

PGL Young Adventure.	Britain, France & Spain.	Co.

Orienteering

PGL Young Adventure.	Britain, France & Spain.	Co.

Rock Climbing and Abseiling

PGL Young Adventure.	Britain, France & Spain.	Co.

Rowing

PGL Young Adventure.	Britain, France & Spain.	Co.

Rugby Union

Muscat Rugby Club.	Oman.	Mag.
S.A.F.	France.	Mag.
Brussels British Rugby Club.	Belgium.	Mag.

Sailing

PGL Young Adventure.	Britain, France & Spain.	Co.
West of Ireland Activity Centre.	Ireland.	Bk.
Camp Duncan.	USA.	Int.
Club Mediterranee.	Europe & North Africa.	Bk.
Lake Powell Resort.	USA.	Int.
Mark Warner.	Corsica, Italy, Sardinia, Greece & Turkey.	Co.
Yacht Crew Register.	Canada.	Int.

See also 'Crew' under 'Work not directly connected to sport'

Self-Defence – Judo, Karate, etc.

PGL Young Adventure.	Britain, France & Spain.	Co.

Shooting
PGL Young Adventure.	Britain, France & Spain.	Co.

Skateboarding
PGL Young Adventure.	Britain, France & Spain.	Co.

Skiing and Snowboarding
Airtours Plc.	Worldwide.	Co.
Alpine Meadows (Lake Tahoe).	USA.	Int.
Aspen.	USA.	Int.
B-Bar Guest Ranch.	USA.	Int.
Badger Pass.	USA.	Int.
Big Sky.	USA.	Int.
Boreal.	USA.	Int.
Breckenridge.	USA.	Int.
Copper Mountain.	USA.	Int.
Cowboy Village.	USA.	Int.
Crested Butte.	USA.	Int.
Crystal Holidays.	Worldwide.	Co.
Crystal Mountain.	USA.	Int.
Eldorada.	USA.	Int.
First Choice Ski.	Europe & North America.	Co.
Flagg Ranch.	USA.	Int.
Heavenly (Lake Tahoe).	USA.	Int.
Hidden Valley.	USA.	Int.
Home Ranch.	USA.	Int.
Hunter Mountain.	USA.	Int.
Keystone.	USA.	Int.
Lone Mountain.	USA.	Int.
Loon Mountain.	USA.	Int.
Mammoth Mountain.	USA.	Int.
Mark Warner.	Italy.	Co.
Mission Ridge.	USA.	Int.
Mount Bachelor.	USA.	Int.
Mount Snow.	USA.	Int.
Northstar.	USA.	Int.
Okemo.	USA.	Int.
PGL Ski Europe.	Austria.	Co.
Purgatory.	USA.	Int.
Roaring Fork.	USA.	Int.
Royal Gorge Cross.	USA.	Int.
Shanty Creek.	USA.	Int.

Ski Esprit.	Switzerland.	News.
Ski Total.	Austria, France & Switzerland.	Mag.
Snowbasin.	USA.	Int.
Snowbird.	USA.	Int.
Soda Springs.	USA.	Int.
Sonnenalp.	USA.	Int.
Steamboat.	USA.	Int.
Stratton Mountain.	USA.	Int.
Sugarbush.	USA.	Int.
Sunday River.	USA.	Int.
Taos.	USA.	Int.
Telluride.	USA.	Int.
Timberline.	USA.	Int.
Vail.	USA.	Int.
Village Camps.	Switzerland.	News.
Waterville Valley.	USA.	Int.
Winter Park.	USA.	Int.
Woodspur Lodge.	USA.	Int.

Soccer

PGL Young Adventure.	Britain, France & Spain.	Co.
Cleveland State University.	USA.	Int.

Softball

PGL Young Adventure.	Britain, France & Spain.	Co.

Surfing

PGL Young Adventure.	Britain, France & Spain.	Co.
Halsbury Travel Ltd.	France, Germany, Spain.	Co.

Swimming, Diving and Life-Saving

PGL Young Adventure.	Britain, France & Spain.	Co.
Camp Duncan.	USA.	Int.
City of Virginia Beach.	USA.	Int.
Mark Warner.	Corsica, Italy, Sardinia, Greece & Turkey.	Co.
Rotfluhhotel.	Austria.	Bk.
University of Kansas.	USA.	Int.
University of Southern California.	USA.	Int.

Squash

PGL Young Adventure.	Britain, France & Spain.	Co.
Squash R. Assoc.	USA.	Int.

Tennis

PGL Young Adventure.	Britain, France & Spain.	Co.
Cleveland State University.	USA.	Int.
Club Mediterranee.	Europe & North Africa.	Bk.
Mark Warner.	Corsica, Italy, Sardinia, Greece & Turkey.	Co.
Tennis Club Zinal.	Switzerland.	Bk.

Volleyball

PGL Young Adventure.	Britain, France & Spain.	Co.

Walking

PGL Young Adventure.	Britain, France & Spain.	Co.
Backroads.	Worldwide.	Int.
Home Ranch.	USA.	Int.
Ramblers Holidays.	Europe & beyond.	Co.
Suntrek Tours.	USA & Mexico.	Int.

Water Skiing

Club Mediterranee.	Europe & North Africa.	Bk.
Halsbury Travel Ltd.	France, Germany & Spain.	Co.
Mark Warner.	Corsica, Italy, Sardinia, Greece & Turkey.	Co.

Weight Training

University of S. California.	USA.	Int.

White Water Rafting

PGL Young Adventure.	Britain, France & Spain.	Co.
Backroads.	Canada.	Int.
Cherokee Adventures Inc.	USA.	Int.

Windsurfing

PGL Young Adventure.	Britain, France & Spain.	Co.
West of Ireland Activity Centre.	Ireland.	Bk.
Canvas Holidays.	Throughout Europe.	Co.
Club Mediterranee.	Europe & North Africa.	Bk.

Halsbury Travel Ltd.	France, Germany & Spain.	Co.
Mark Warner.	Corsica, Italy, Sardinia, Greece & Turkey.	Co.

WORK NOT DIRECTLY CONNECTED TO YOUR SPORT

Accounting and Auditing

Grand Canyon National Park.	USA.	Int.
Lake Powell Resort.	USA.	Int.
The Mountain Trading Company.	France.	Mag.
United States Tennis Association.	USA.	Int.

Activity Organiser

PGL Young Adventure.	Britain, France & Spain.	Co.
Airtours Plc.	Worldwide.	Co.
Camp Duncan.	USA.	Int.
Colossus Beach Hotel.	Greece.	Bk.
Eurocamp.	Throughout Europe.	Co.
Home Ranch.	USA.	Int.
Lazy H Ranch.	USA.	Int.

Administration

Cowboy Village.	USA.	Int.
Home Ranch.	USA.	Int.
Lost Creek Ranch.	USA.	Int.
Sea Pines Resort.	USA.	Int.

Alpine Studies Co-ordinators

PGL Ski Europe.	France.	Co.

Announcer/Commentator

La Cross Bobcats.	USA.	Int.

Attendants – Sports Centres, Golf Courses, Tennis Courts, etc.

Alpine Meadows Ski Resort.	USA.	Int.
Aspen Lodge and Estes Park.	USA.	Int.
Lake Powell Resort.	USA.	Int.

Bar Staff

PGL Young Adventure.	Britain, France & Spain.	Co.
The Brown Rock Company.	France.	Mag.

Cowboy Village.	USA.	Int.
Kiawah Island Resort.	USA.	Int.
Lake Powell Resort.	USA.	Int.

Cashiers and Sales Assistants

Alpine Meadows Ski Resort.	USA.	Int.
Cowboy Village.	USA.	Int.
Grand Canyon National Park.	USA.	Int.
Heavenly Ski Resort.	USA.	Int.
Home Ranch.	USA.	Int.
Kiawah Island Resort.	USA.	Int.
Lake Powell Resort.	USA.	Int.
Sea Pines Resort.	USA.	Int.

Camp Counselling

BUNAC.	USA.	Int.
Camp America.	USA.	Int.
Camp Duncan.	USA.	Int.

Chalet Work

Cordon Rouge.	France.	Mag.
Le Ski.	France.	Mag.
Silver Ski Holidays.	France.	Mag.
Ski Beat.	France.	Mag.
Ski Total.	Austria, France & Switzerland.	Mag.
Village Camps.	Switzerland.	Mag.

Chefs, Cooks, Caterers and Kitchen Assistants

Aspen Lodge And Estes Park.	USA.	Int.
B-Bar Guest Ranch.	USA.	Int.
The Brown Rock Company.	France.	Mag.
Camp Duncan.	USA.	Int.
Clear Creek Ranch.	USA.	Int.
Cowboy Village.	USA.	Int.
Drowsy Water Ranch.	USA.	Int.
Grand Canyon National Park.	USA.	Int.
Home Ranch.	USA.	Int.
Hooligan Ranch.	USA.	Int.
Kiawah Island Resort.	USA.	Int.
Lake Powell Resort.	USA.	Int.
Lazy H Ranch.	USA.	Int.

Lit'le Mary Ranch.	USA.	Int.
Lone Mount Ranch.	USA.	Int.
Lost Creek Ranch.	USA.	Int.
The Mountain Trading Company.	France.	Mag.
PGL Young Adventure.	France.	Co.
Silver Ski Holidays.	France.	Mag.
Ski Total.	Austria, France & Switzerland.	Mag.
Village Camps.	Switzerland.	Mag.
Yacht Crew Register.	Canada.	Int.

Computers and Information Technology

PGL Young Adventure.	Britain, France & Spain.	Co.
Angel Fire Resort.	USA.	Int.

Co-ordinators

Cleveland State University.	USA.	Int.
Georgia Games.	USA.	Int.
US Tennis Association.	USA.	Int.

Crew

Bombard Balloon Adventures.	USA.	Bk.
European Waterways.	France & Spain.	Co.
Yacht Crew Register.	Canada.	Int.

Driving

HGV or PSV licence often required, and ability to cope with mechanical breakdowns.

PGL Young Adventure.	Britain, France & Spain.	Co.
Alpine Meadows Ski Resort.	USA.	Int.
Clear Creek Ranch.	USA.	Int.
Cowboy Village.	USA.	Int.
Grand Canyon National Park.	USA.	Int.
Great Alaska Fish Camp.	USA.	Int.
Heavenly Ski Resort.	USA.	Int.
Kiawah Island Resort.	USA.	Int.
Lake Powell Resort.	USA.	Int.
Mark Warner.	Corsica, Italy, Sardinia, Greece & Turkey.	Co.
Telluride Ski Resort.	USA.	Int.

Evening Entertainers

*Companies often require previous experience in these positions, &
sometimes ability to speak local language.*

Airtours Plc.	Worldwide.	Co.
The Brown Rock Company	France.	Mag.
Colossus Beach Hotel.	Greece.	Bk.

Farrier

Drowsy Water Ranch.	USA.	Int.

Fire Safety Officer

Grand Canyon National Park.	USA.	Int.

First Aiders

PGL Young Adventure.	Britain, France & Spain.	Co.

Gardening and Landscaping

B-Bar Guest Ranch.	USA.	Int.

Groundsmen

Grand Canyon National Park.	USA.	Int.
Kiawah Island Resort.	USA.	Int.
Sea Pines Resort.	USA.	Int.

Hotel Work

Mark Warner.	Corsica, Italy, Sardinia, Greece & Turkey.	Co.
Aspen Lodge and Estes Park.	USA.	Int.
Club Mediterranee.	Europe & North Africa.	Bk.
Crystal Holidays.	Worldwide.	Co.
Lake Powell Resort.	USA.	Int.

Housekeeper

Aspen Lodge and Estes Park.	USA.	Int.
B-Bar Guest Ranch.	USA.	Int.
Clear Creek Ranch.	USA.	Int.
Cowboy Village.	USA.	Int.
Drowsy Water Ranch.	USA.	Int.
Grand Canyon National Park.	USA.	Int.
Home Ranch.	USA.	Int.
Kiawah Island Resort.	USA.	Int.
Lake Powell Resort.	USA.	Int.

Lazy H Ranch.	USA.	Int.
Lazy L&B Ranch.	USA.	Int.
Lost Creek Ranch.	USA.	Int.
Sea Pines Resort.	USA.	Int.
Vista Verde Ranch.	USA.	Int.

Language Teaching

PGL Young Adventure.	Britain, France & Spain.	Co.

Maintenance Staff

Alpine Meadows Ski Resort.	USA.	Int.
Aspen Lodge and Estes Park.	USA.	Int.
Camp Duncan.	USA.	Int.
Cowboy Village.	USA.	Int.
Drowsy Water Ranch.	USA.	Int.
French Country Camping (Bikes).	France.	Mag.
Grand Canyon National Park.	USA.	Int.
Heavenly Ski Resort.	USA.	Int.
Home Ranch.	USA.	Int.
Kiawah Island Resort.	USA.	Int.
Lake Powell Resort.	USA.	Int.
Lost Creek Ranch.	USA.	Int.
Ski Total.	Austria, France & Switzerland.	Mag.
Telluride Ski Resort.	USA.	Int.

Management

Camp Duncan.	USA.	Int.
Dubuquee University.	USA.	Int.
Global Apparel.	USA.	Int.
Grand Canyon National Park.	USA.	Int.
Kiawah Island Resort.	USA.	Int.
La Cross Bobcats.	USA.	Int.
Tampa Bay Mutiny.	USA.	Int.
Professional Cycling League.	USA.	Int.
Sports Arena Director.	USA.	Int.
Sports Media Manager.	USA.	Int.
Ski Total	Austria, France & Switzerland.	Mag.
West Michigan Whitecaps.	USA.	Int.
University of North Carolina.	USA.	Int.
US Squash Racquets Assoc.	USA.	Int.

Village Camps.	Switzerland.	News.

Nannies

Club Mediterranee.	Europe & North Africa.	Bk.
Le Ski.	France.	Mag.
Ski Esprit.	Switzerland.	News.
Mark Warner.	Corsica, Italy, Sardinia, Greece & Turkey.	Co.

Nurses

PGL Young Adventure.	Britain, France & Spain.	Co.
Camp Duncan.	USA.	Int.
Village Camps.	Switzerland.	Mag.

Physiotherapists

VSO.	Sri Lanka.	News.
VSO.	Papua New Guinea.	News.

Rescue Boat Drivers

PGL Young Adventure.	Britain, France & Spain.	Co.

Resort Reps, Couriers, etc.

Airtours Plc.	Worldwide.	Co.
Grand Canyon National Park.	USA.	Int.
Club Mediterranee.	Europe & North Africa.	Bk.
Crystal Holidays.	Worldwide.	Co.
Eurocamp.	Throughout Europe.	Co.

Sales Reps

Tampa Bay Rowdies.	USA.	Int.
Telluride Ski Resort.	USA.	Int.
Sports Equipment International.	USA.	Int.
Hilton Heat.	USA.	Int.
Western Pro Hockey League.	USA.	Int.

Security Staff

The Brown Rock Company.	France.	Mag.

Sports Photographers

Dallas.	USA.	Int.
Fort Worth.	USA.	Int.

Sports Science
Cleminson University.	USA.	Int.

Stores Assistants
PGL Young Adventure.	Britain, France & Spain.	Co.
Grand Canyon National Park.	USA.	Int.

Teachers
PGL Young Adventure.	Britain, France & Spain.	Co.

Video Film Making
PGL Young Adventure.	Britain, France & Spain.	Co.
Human Resources & Kinetics.	USA.	Int.

Waitresses, Waiters
Aspen Lodge and Estes Park.	USA.	Int.
The Brown Rock Company.	France.	Mag.
Cowboy Village.	USA.	Int.
Drowsy Water Ranch.	USA.	Int.
Home Ranch.	USA.	Int.
Kiawah Island Resort.	USA.	Int.
Lone Mount Ranch.	USA.	Int.
Lost Creek Ranch.	USA.	Int.
Sea Pines Resort.	USA.	Int.
Vista Verde Ranch.	USA.	Int.

Writer
United States Tennis Association.	USA.	Int.

Youth Leaders
PGL Young Adventure.	Britain, France & Spain.	Co.

5

Making Contact

This chapter lists the addresses and telephone numbers of most of the major UK sports governing bodies and national organisers. If you require one that is not contained in this list then contact the United Kingdom Sports Council, Walkenden House, 3 Melton Street, London NW1 2EB, Tel. (0171) 380 8000, and they will advise.

CONTACTING YOUR NATIONAL GOVERNING BODY

Aerobics and Fitness
Chairman, Mrs J. Moore, The Keep-Fit Association,
Francis House, Francis Street, London, SW1P 1DE.
Tel. (0171) 233 8898
and
Secretary, The Exercise Association of England Ltd.,
Unit 4, Angel Gate, City Road, London, EC1V 2PT.
Tel. (0171) 278 0811

Angling
Chief Administration Officer, National Federation of Anglers,
Egginton Junction, Egginton, Derbyshire, DE65 6GU.
Tel. (01283) 734735

Archery
Chief Executive, Mr J.S. Middleton, Grand National Archery Society,
7th Street, National Agricultural Centre, Stoneleigh, Kenilworth, Warwickshire, CV8 2LG.
Tel. (01203) 696631

Athletics
Mr D. R. Moorcroft MBE, Chief Executive, Athletics UK,
30A Harborne Road, Edgbaston, Birmingham B15 3AA.
Tel. (0121) 466 5098

Badminton
Chief Executive, Mr S. Baddeley, Badminton Association of England Ltd,
Bradwell Rd, Loughton Lodge, Milton Keynes, MK8 9LA.
Tel. (01908) 268400

Basketball
Chief Executive, Mr Stephen Catton, English Basketball Association,
48 Bradford Road, Stanningly, Leeds, LS28 6DF.
Tel. (0113) 236 1020

Billiards and Snooker
Co-ordinator, Miss F. Broad, English Association for Billiards and Snooker,
27 Oakfield Road, Bristol, BS8 2AT.
Tel. (0117) 923 9600

Boxing
Secretary, Mr C. Brown, The Amateur Boxing Association of England Ltd.,
Crystal Palace, Norwood, London, SE19 2BB.
Tel. (0181) 778 0935

Canoeing
Chief Executive, Mr P. Owen, British Canoe Union,
Adbolton Lane, West Bridgford, Nottingham, NG2 5AS.
Tel. (0115) 982 1100

Caving
Secretary, Mr S. Baguley, National Caving Association,
White Lion House, Ynys Uchaf, Ystradgynlais, Swansea, SA9 1RW.
Tel. (01639) 849519

Cricket
National Development Manager, Mr T.N. Bates, England and Wales Cricket Board,
Lord's Cricket Ground, London, NW8 8QZ.
Tel. (0171) 432 1200

Cycling
Chief Executive, Mr J. Hendry, British Cycling Federation,
National Cycling Centre, Stuart St, Manchester, M11 4DQ.
Tel. (0161) 230 2301

Equestrianism
British Horse Society, Chief Executive Officer, Col. T.J.S. Eastwood,
Stoneleigh Park, Kenilworth, Warwickshire, CV8 2LR.
Tel. (01203) 696697
and
The Jockey Club,
42 Portman Square, London, W1H 0EN.
Tel. (0171) 486 4921

Fencing
Ms G.M. Kinneally, British Fencing Association,
1 Barons Gate, 33 Rothschild Road, London, W4 5HT.
Tel. (0181) 742 3032

Golf
Secretary, Mr P.M. Baxter, English Golf Union,
The National Golf Centre, Woodhall Spa, Lincs., LN10 6PH.
Tel. (01526) 354500
or
The PGA Training Dept., National Headquarters,
The Belfry, Sutton Coldfield, West Midlands, B76 9PT.
Tel. (01675) 470333
or
The PGA European Tour, Wentworth Club, Virginia Water,
Surrey, GU25 4LS.
Tel. (01344) 842881

Gymnastics
General Secretary, Mr D. Minnery, British Gymnastics,
Ford Hall, Lilleshall, Newport, Shropshire, TF10 9NB.
Tel. (01952) 820330

Hang Gliding and Paragliding
Secretary, Ms J. Burdett, British Hang Gliding and Paragliding
Association,
The Old School Room, Loughborough Road, Leicester, LE4 5PJ.
Tel. (0116) 261 1322

Hockey
Administrator, Ms T. Willis, English Hockey Association,
The Stadium, Silbury Boulevard, Milton Keynes, MK9 1HA.
Tel. (01908) 544644

Ice Hockey
Technical Director, Mr N. Toeman, British Ice Hockey Association,
National Sports Centre, Adbolton Lane, Holme Pierrepont,
Nottingham, NG12 2LU.
Tel. (0115) 982 1515

Judo
Office Manager, Ms S. Startin, British Judo Association,
7a Rutland Street, Leicester, LE1 1RB.
Tel. (0116) 255 9669

Karate
General Secretary, Mr G. Wallace, English Karate Governing Body,
629B High Road, Seven Kings, Essex, IG3 8RB.
Tel. (0181) 599 0711

Martial Arts
The Martial Arts Commission,
15 Deptford Broadway, London, SE8 4PA.

Motorsports
Chief Executive, Mr J. Quenby, Motorsport House,
Riverside Park, Colnbrook, Slough, SL3 0HG.
Tel. (01753) 681736

Mountain Biking
Development Officer, Mr B. Johnson, British Mountain Biking
Association,
National Cycling Centre, Stuart St, Manchester, M11 4DQ.
Tel. (0161) 230 2301

Netball
Chief Executive, Mrs E.M. Nicholl, All England Netball Association,
9 Paynes Park, Hitchin, Herts. SG5 1EH.
Tel. (01462) 442344

Orienteering
The Secretary General, British Orienteering Federation,
Riversdale, Dale Road North, Darley Dale, Matlock, Derby, DE4
2HX.
Tel. (01629) 734042

Parachuting
Technical Officer, Mr A.K. Butler, British Parachute Association,
5 Wharf Way, Glen Parva, Leicester, LE2 9TF
Tel. (0116) 278 5271

Rowing
National Manager, Mrs R.E. Napp, Amateur Rowing Association,
The Priory, 6 Lower Mall, Hammersmith, London, W6 9DJ.
Tel. (0181) 748 3632

Rugby League
Chief Executive, Mr M.F. Oldroyd, British Amateur Rugby League Association,
4 New North Parade, Huddersfield, HD1 5JP.
Tel. (01484) 544131

Rugby Union
Secretary, Rugby Football Union,
Twickenham, Middlesex, TW1 1DZ.
Tel. (0181) 892 8161

Sailing
Manager, Mr J. White, Royal Yachting Association,
Romsey Road, Eastleigh, Hampshire, SO50 9YA.
Tel. (01703) 627400

Shooting
Chief Executive, Lt Col. C.C.C. Cheshire OBE, National Rifle Association,
Bisley Camp, Brookwood, Woking, Surrey, GU24 0PB.
Tel. (01483) 797777

Skiing and Snowboarding
Chief Executive, Mr M. Jardine, British Ski and Snowboard Federation,
258 Main Street, East Calder, Livingston, West Lothian, EH53 0EE.
Tel. (01506) 884343
and
Chief Executive, Mrs D. King, English Ski Council,
Area Library Building, Queensway Mall, The Combow, Halesowen, B63 4AJ.
Tel. (0121) 501 2314

Soccer
Chief Executive, The Football Association,
16 Lancaster Gate, London, W2 3LW.
Tel. (0171) 262 4542

Squash
General Secretary, Mr N. Moore, Squash Racquets Association,
P.O. Box 1106, London, W3 0ZD.
Tel. (0181) 746 1616

Surfing
Administrator, Mr C.K. Wilson, British Surfing Association,
Champions Yard, Penzance, Cornwall, TR18 2TA.
Tel. (01736) 360250

Swimming
Chief Executive, Mr D. Sparkes, Amateur Swimming Association,
Derby Square, Loughborough, LE11 5AL.
Tel. (01509) 618700

Table Tennis
General Secretary, Mr R. Sinclair, English Table Tennis Association,
3rd Floor, Queensbury House, Havelock Road, Hastings, TN34 1HF.
Tel. (01424) 722525

Tennis
Secretary, Mr J.C.U. James, The Lawn Tennis Association,
The Queens Club, West Kensington, London, W14 9EG.
Tel. (0171) 381 7000

Tenpin Bowling
Chairman, Mrs P. White, British Tenpin Bowling Association,
114 Balfour Road, Ilford, Essex, IG1 4JD.
Tel. (0181) 478 1745

Trampolining
Secretary, Mr R.C. Walker, British Trampoline Federation,
146 College Road, Harrow, HA1 1BH.
Tel. (0181) 863 7278

Volleyball
Chief Executive Officer, Mrs Gillian Harrison, English Volleyball
Association,
27 South Road, West Bridgford, Nottingham, NG2 7AG.
Tel. (0115) 981 6324

Water Skiing
Executive Officer, Ms G. Hill, British Water Ski Federation,
390 City Road, London, EC1V 2QA.
Tel. (0171) 833 2855

Weight Lifting
Secretary, Mrs J. Gaul, British Amateur Weight Lifters Association,
Grosvenor House, 131 Hurst Street, Oxford, OX4 1HE.
Tel. (01865) 200339

Windsurfing
Manager, Mr J. White, Royal Yachting Association,
Romsey Road, Eastleigh, Hampshire, SO50 9YA.
Tel. (01703) 627400

WRITING TO YOUR NATIONAL GOVERNING BODY

When writing to your sports governing body always use a typewriter or wordprocessor and check what you've written as well as using the spellchecker. Include all the important information like your name, address, telephone number, the location that you are interested in working in and your qualifications, if you want your application to be processed quickly.

A sample letter is shown in Figure 5 and is included merely as a straightforward example of what is required. Adapt it in any way that you consider to be appropriate.

CONTACTING A NATIONAL ORGANISING BODY

The Sports Council
Information Centre, 16 Upper Woburn Place, London, WC1H 0QP.
Tel. (0171) 273 1500

The National Coaching Foundation
Information Service,
114 Cardigan Road, Headingley, Leeds, LS6 3BJ.
Tel. (0113) 274 4802

British Universities Sports Association
Tel. (0171) 357 8555

The National Association for Outdoor Education
12 St Andrews Churchyard, Penrith, Cumbria CA11 7YE.
Tel. (01768) 865113

The UK Outdoor Institute
Eastgate House, Princeshay, Exeter, EX1 1LY.
Tel. (01392) 72372

Royal Life Saving Society UK
Ms H. Bradley, River House, High Street, Broom, B50 4HN.
Tel. (01789) 773994

The British Red Cross
National HQ, 9 Grosvenor Crescent, London, SW1.
Tel. (0171) 235 5454

St John Ambulance
National HQ, 1 Grosvenor Crescent, London, SW1.
Tel. (0171) 258 3456

Peter Stevens,
123 The High Street,
Smallborough,
London.
EW3 4LK
Tel: 01234 567890

29 February 2002

Mr J. Newbody,
The National Coach,
Anysports Headquarters.

Dear Mr Newbody,
I am interested in playing anysports in a European country for the coming season and I wondered if you might be able to suggest someone I can contact or advise me on my best course of action. I have an 'A' level in German, which I also speak fluently, so my preferred countries are Austria, Germany or Switzerland but I am happy to apply to other EEC countries as well.

For the past two years I have played in the Southern League Division One for Smallborough United and last season I was voted their Most Valued Player. It is my intention to gain experience whilst working abroad before applying to university to study for a sports-related degree.

I would be very grateful for your assistance but if you are unable to help could you please send me the addresses of the anysports governing bodies in Austria, Germany and Switzerland.

I look forward to hearing from you. Thank you for your assistance.

Yours sincerely,

Peter Stevens

Peter Stevens

Fig. 5.   Sample letter to a national governing body.

The Chartered Society of Physiotherapy
14 Bedford Row, London, WC1R 4ED.

Association of Chartered Physiotherapists in Sports Medicine
14 Mayfield Court, Moseley, Birmingham, B13 9UD.

The Institute of Leisure and Amenity Management
ILAM House, Lower Basildon, Reading, Berkshire, RG8 9NE.

The Institute of Baths and Recreational Management
IBRM, Giffard House, 36 Sherrard Street, Melton Mowbray, Leics.,
LE13 1XJ.

The Institute of Professional Sport
Francis Street, London, SW1P 1DE.
Tel. (0171) 828 3163

The City and Guilds of London Institute
1 Giltspur Street, London, EC1A.
Tel. (0171) 294 2468

Business and Technician Education Council (BTEC)
Central House, Upper Woburn Place, London, WC1 0HH.
Tel. (0171) 388 3288

Scottish Vocational Education Council (SCOTVEC)
Hanover House, 24 Douglas Street, Glasgow, G2 7NQ.
Tel. (0141) 248 7900

You might need to write a letter as shown in Figure 6 for one of many
reasons. This one is included as an example of how to acquire more
qualifications.

CONTACTING A UNIVERSITY OFFERING SPORTS SCHOLAR-SHIPS IN THE UK

Some UK universities offer sports scholarships but there is no
national scheme for this and it is entirely down to individual universities. It is nowhere near as common or as financially rewarding as it
is in the USA. More specific details are in Chapter Two.

Aberdeen University
Department of Physical Education,
University Road, Aberdeen, AB9 2UW.
Tel. (01224) 272314

Bristol University
Director of Sport, Exercise and Health Science,
34 West Park, Clifton, Bristol, BS8 2LU.
Tel. (0117) 928 8810

Peter Stevens,
123 The High Street,
Smallborough,
London.
EW3 4LK.
Tel: 01234 567890
29 February 2002

The British Red Cross,
National Headquarters,
9 Grosvenor Crescent,
London, SW1.

Dear Sir,
I am interested in taking a course that will lead to becoming qualified in first aid. Unfortunately I haven't been able to obtain this information from either my local library or through local newspapers.

Could you please provide me with the contact address of the local organiser of these courses and, if possible, let me know the dates they run and the cost of enrolment.

Thank you for your assistance.

Yours faithfully,

Peter Stevens

Peter Stevens

Fig. 6. Sample letter to a national organising body.

Brunel University, West London
Department of Sport Sciences,
Osterley Campus, Borough Road, Isleworth, Middlesex, TW7 5DU.
Tel. (0181) 891 0121

Coventry University
Jane Howard,
Room F120, Coventry University, CV1 5FJ.
Tel. (01203) 838977

De Montford University
Scholarship Coordinator,
21 Landsdowne Road, Bedford, MK40 2BZ.

Durham University
Director of Sport,
The Graham Sports Centre, Maiden Castle, Durham, DH1 3SE.
Tel. (0191) 374 2000

Edinburgh University
Director of PE,
46 Pleasance, Edinburgh, EH8 9TJ.
Tel. (0131) 650 2580

Exeter University
Athletic Union, Cornwall, House, St German's Road, Exeter, EX4 6TG.
Tel. (01392) 279852

Heriot–Watt University
Centre for Sport and Exercise, Riccarton, Edinburgh, EH14 4AS.
Tel. (0131) 449 5111 ext. 4050

Landsdowne College
7 Palace Gate, London, W8 5LS.
Tel. (0171) 581 3307

Leeds Metropolitan University
Margaret Talbot, University Head of Sport,
Beckett Park Campus, Leeds, LS6 3QS.
Tel. (0113) 283 7431

Loughborough University
Loughborough, Leics., LE11 3TU.
Tel. (01509) 263171

Oxford University
The Richard Blackwell Scholarship Trust,
50 Broad Street, Oxford, OX1 3BQ.
Tel. (01865) 792792

Trinity and All Saints College (TASC)
Students Union, Brownberrie Lane, Horsforth, Leeds, LS18 5HD.
Tel. (0113) 239 0201

Worcester College
Malcolm Armstrong, Head of Sports Studies,
Henwick Grove, Worcester, WR2 6AJ.
Tel. (01905) 748080

University of Bath
Department of Sports Development and Recreation,
Claverton Down, Bath, BA2 7AY.
Tel. (01225) 826656 or 826417

University of Birmingham
Edgbaston, Birmingham, B15 2TT.
Tel. (0121) 414 3344

University of Brighton
Recreation Office, Falmer, Brighton, BN1 3PH.
Tel. (01273) 643521

University College of Swansea
Singleton Park, Swansea, SA2 8PP.
Tel. (01792) 205678

University of Dundee
Director of PE, Nethergate, Dundee, DD1 4NP.
Tel. (01382) 344121

University of Glasgow
Department of Physical Education and Sports Sciences,
Stevenson Building, 64 Oakfield Avenue, Glasgow, G12 8LT.
Tel. (0141) 339 8855 ext. 4540

University of Newcastle
Kings Walk, Newcastle upon Tyne, NE1 7RU.
Tel. (0191) 222 6000

University of Northumbria
Director of Sport,
Wynne Jones Centre, Newcastle upon Tyne, NE1 8ST.
Tel. (0191) 227 4329

University of St. Andrews
Dr M. Farrally Dept of PE,
St Leonards Road, St Andrews, Fife, KY16 9DY.
Tel. (01334) 76161

University of Salford
The Crescent, Salford, Lancs., M5 4WT.
Tel. (0161) 745 5000

University of Stirling
Alan Nicholls, Centre for PE and Sport, Stirling, FK9 4LA.
Tel. (01786) 466901

University of Strathclyde
Sports Association, 90 John Street, Glasgow, G1 1JH.
Tel. (0141) 552 5320

University of Surrey
Linguistic and International Studies Department,
University of Surrey, Guildford.

University of Teesside
Sport and Recreation Unit, Middlesbrough, Cleveland, TS1 3BA.
Tel. (01642) 342267

University of Ulster
Director of Sport and Recreation, Shore Road, Newtownabbey,
Northern Ireland, BT37 0QB.

University of Wales (UWIC)
Ian Campbell, Athletic Union, Cyncoed, Cardiff, CF2 6XD.
Tel. (01222) 506953

CONTACTING A UNIVERSITY OFFERING SPORTS SCHOLARSHIPS OVERSEAS

The number of Universities and Colleges around the world offering
sports scholarships are so numerous that to include details of them
all would be beyond the scope of this book.

However, information on opportunities in the USA can be
obtained by reading *Sports Scholarships and College Programs in the
USA*; editor Ron Walker by Petersons Guides. This can be borrowed
from most main libraries or purchased from the UK distributor:
Vacation Work Publications.

6

Ensuring You Have the Necessary Qualifications

There are no qualifications required for a professional playing career in any sport, just outstanding ability. Unfortunately, though, successful careers can be cut short at any time through injury. Therefore it would be a foolish person who ignores gaining qualifications or experience that will help them get a job when their sporting career is over. Many soccer clubs acknowledge this and insist that their apprentice professionals study for educational qualifications.

It is advisable to study for recognised qualifications awarded by reputable bodies. Some of these are detailed below. If you want to pursue a career in coaching or instructing, it would be advisable to hold a coaching certificate. Details of these follow under 'Acquiring national coaching awards'.

To gain a position in certain careers you need to study for a certificate or diploma organised by a recognised body within that profession. Details are given below under 'Gaining professional qualifications'. A 'vocational' qualification concentrates on job-related skills and knowledge compared to an 'academic' qualification which reflects a depth of study in a much narrower subject area.

OBTAINING GENERAL QUALIFICATIONS

GCSE

Normally taken when you are at school, so the majority of young people should now have examination passes in a number of subjects at this level. If you feel however that you should have done better, for whatever reason, all is not lost. Most towns have at least one facility where you can resit or take further examinations. Look them up in the *Yellow Pages* telephone directory under 'Schools and colleges'.

You may think it's a little unjust but details of these qualifications will be needed for the rest of your working life. Even when applying for a new job when aged 50 the employer will ask you what school examination passes you achieved. So it is very important that you do as well as you can in these. Some of you will have succeeded at GCSE and obtained good grades at 'A' level too. This is an added bonus as more opportunities will be available to you.

Once you have left school – with or without GCSE qualifications – there is a plethora of available courses, many of them sports related, that you may take.

The range and number of these courses can be quite confusing, so, in an attempt to simplify them, the following general rules can be applied under the assumption that we're confining ourselves to sports-related study:

• City and Guilds courses offer, amongst other things, opportunities for work in Sports Centres.

• Business and Technician Education Council (BTEC) courses are aimed at people who want the option of going into Higher Education sports studies.

• National Vocational Qualification (NVQ) courses offer a practical, work-based type of study and are popular with those who are interested in working in tourism.

This is a very simplified explanation of these courses and there is a significant amount of overlap and integration between them. You may take a qualification with one examining body, but have to transfer to a different one to achieve the final diploma that you require. For example, the BTEC First Diploma in Sports Studies qualifies you to go on to the General National Vocational Qualification (GNVQ) in Leisure and Tourism, as well as the BTEC National Diploma in Sports Studies.

All this can be very confusing and, in order to make it clearer, further details of these awards are given below.

City and Guilds

This is a vocationally based qualification with a small amount of academic content that can be passed at four different levels – Parts 1, 2, 3, and 4, – with the last being the hardest to pass and, obviously, the most academically demanding. By comparison, Part 1 is very practical and easier to pass. You should not need any qualifications to enrol on these courses, although this may be at the discretion of your local college.

These awards are long established and recognised by all British-owned companies abroad. Many foreign companies also recognise them but this will depend on where you are seeking employment.

If you would like more information contact your local school or college or The City and Guilds Institute – see Chapter 5. Their most popular course is 'Recreation and Leisure Studies' so expect competition if you are applying for it.

BTEC

BTEC, which stands for the Business and Technician Education Council, concerns itself with numerous vocational qualifications including 'Leisure, Recreation, and Management'. These qualifications are recognised, in a similar fashion to the City and Guilds, throughout Britain and by British-owned companies abroad – although in Scotland they have their own equivalent version called the SCOTVEC (Scottish Vocational Education Council).

BTEC has five levels of qualification ranging from Level One – the First Diploma or Certificate, up to Level Five – the Continuing Education Certificate (CEC). The BTEC First Diploma is equivalent to City and Guilds Part 2. The BTEC Level Three is equivalent to City and Guilds Part 4 and is also considered equivalent to the first year of a degree course.

No educational qualifications are normally required to enrol for a First Diploma level course. Most colleges accept candidates on the strength of their interview and references from their school.

Further information can be obtained by contacting your local school or college, the BTEC or SCOTVEC bodies (see Chapter 5), or reading some of the relevant books in the Further Reading section. *A Guide to Jobs and Qualifications in Sport and Recreation* by John Potter/ILAM is particularly recommended.

NVQ/GNVQ

The National Vocational Qualification, and the SVQ in Scotland, were originally intended to replace the BTEC and the City and Guilds and, for a while, there was a confusing overlap between them all. This appears to have been rectified to some extent by the examining boards specialising in different fields so, if your career choice is to work in tourism, then you would initially take an NVQ course.

The NVQ awards tend to be more practical 'hands on' courses, whereas you can take a more academic, theoretical level of award by enrolling on a GNVQ course.

More advanced awards

There are other, higher-level, qualifications offered as an alternative to those covered thus far but you need to have some of the previously detailed qualifications before being considered for them. You can get information on these more advanced courses from your school, college or course tutor.

GAINING PROFESSIONAL QUALIFICATIONS

Once you have secured work, promotion is often based on experience plus the attainment of higher or professional qualifications. You could progress by attaining a Higher National Diploma, a Higher National Certificate, the Certificate in Management Studies (CMS), the ILAM Certificate in Leisure Operations, the Continuing Education Certificate (CEC), the ILAM Certificate in Leisure Management, the National Examination Board for Supervisory Management (NEBSM), university degree, postgraduate diploma, Masters degree, doctorate, etc. – the list continues to expand at a rapid pace every year.

Most employers have their own personnel department who will advise you on your own career development. If you need further advice then read *A Guide to Jobs and Qualifications in Sport and Recreation* by John Potter/ILAM or look at other relevant books in the Further Reading section. You should also contact your local school, college or career advisors.

ACQUIRING NATIONAL COACHING AWARDS

Many 'beginners' level awards are quite easy to achieve, aren't too time consuming and are also quite inexpensive.

For example, a Club Coach Level One course in athletics is often held over four days. This normally covers two weekends but it varies in different parts of the country. The course structure contains both practical and theory sessions.

When the initial part of the course is successfully completed the prospective coach has to conduct 15 coaching sessions supervised by another qualified coach. Theoretically, if a candidate coached five sessions a week he could become fully qualified in less than five weeks. The cost of this award varies according to the facilities available around the regions but it is still minimal.

If you are interested in applying for a coaching award you should refer to the list of award organisers in Chapter 5 and there is more information on them later in this chapter.

ADDING OTHER LESS FORMAL QUALIFICATIONS

Many employers are just as impressed by applicants who hold other types of qualifications as they often reflect personal qualities not always found in academic or vocational successes.

Driving licence

Many employers expect their employees to hold a driving licence and, for insurance purposes, they often prefer the holder to be over 21 (in some cases over 25) and have no convictions. Holding this simple qualification not only enhances your own lifestyle but also opens up a multitude of job opportunities to you.

First aid

The basic first aid certificate is quite easy to pass and is highly valued by employers. They feel more at ease knowing that their staff are able to handle accidents and emergencies.

Employment agencies often stipulate that candidates must possess first aid qualifications whilst others, the leisure and tourism industry for example, like to state in their glossy brochures that all their staff possess first aid certificates.

If you would like to take one of these awards, or would simply like more information, then look up the address and telephone number of your local Red Cross or St John Ambulance organisations in the telephone directory. If you can't locate them by this method, details of their head offices are given in Chapter 5.

Life saving

Awards in life saving are absolutely essential if you are going to be involved with instructing or assisting with any watersports.

It is also looked on favourably by most other sports-oriented employers as it offers greater flexibility in the type of work you are able to do for them. Even if you are only applying to hire out deckchairs on a beach, holding one of these awards will tip the scales in your favour during the interview.

If you would like to take this award then contact your local swimming baths for details. Their telephone number will be your local directory. Alternatively you can contact the head office of the Royal Life Saving Society. Details of this are given in Chapter 5.

Languages

If you intend to work abroad, speaking the language has a most distinct advantage. Most positions of responsibility are usually advertised with this as a prerequisite for applying. Not all employers, however, ask for formal qualifications. They might ask merely for an ability to speak the language in which case you must expect to be tested during the interview.

Even if you do not speak the language before applying all is not lost. Put the application in, and then start cramming up by using a phrase book. If you are given an interview tell the interviewer that your command of the language is only basic but that you are working to improve it. If you get the job then enrol on a local language course or keep ploughing through the phrase books. With even just a basic ability you will improve in leaps and bounds once you are living in that country.

Other less formal qualifications

Almost any qualification is worth putting down on the application form or CV that you send to an employer. Obviously, though, these will be more useful if they relate directly to the work that you are going to do. For example, a qualification as a mechanic would be advantageous for someone who is applying for a driving job with a holiday company.

However, even if you think your qualification might not be relevant, still put it down as this just might help to get you the job. You never know, the company who employs you as a lifeguard at their swimming pool might also be looking for someone who has computer skills to help cope with the administrative aspects of the job.

LOOKING AFTER YOUR REFERENCES AND TESTIMONIALS

References are asked for by all employers and are provided by referees nominated by you. They are confidential and you rarely see them. Testimonials are 'open' references that you can get from someone in authority – teacher, youth worker, sports coach – and are either included in your application or shown during the interview. If you have either of these in your possession it is vital that you keep them in good condition for future use. Remember that this is what impresses an employer and can often be the difference between being called for interview or having your application thrown in the bin.

SUMMARY

QUALIFICATIONS
- Make sure your qualifications are suitable for the employment that you seek.
- Rectify any deficiencies by going on courses.
- Acquire the easier, less formal, qualifications like first aid. it might just tip the scales in your favour.

REFERENCES and
TESTIMONIALS
- References and testimonials are very important. Get good ones and keep them safe and clean

LANGUAGE
- If you intend working abroad, start to learn the language and let prospective employers know this.

7

Securing the Job

MAKING THE INITIAL CONTACT

Once you have found a job or position that is of interest to you your next task is to contact the person who advertised it. If you are applying to a big company they will probably have their own application form and you simply write a brief letter to the person named asking for one. Examples of this type of letter and a company application form are given later in this chapter.

However, if you are writing to an employer or smaller company who don't produce their own application form then use the following procedure.

Write to them personally and under no circumstances send them a standard obviously duplicated letter. Most employers would take this as a sign that you are not particularly interested in their job but simply after any work that comes along. Figure 7 is an example of a letter to a small company, in this case based in France. If you are fluent in French, write this letter in French to prove you have linguistic skills.

Also send them your curriculum vitae (CV), the names of referees and any testimonials you have and a recent photograph, even if they are not asked for. This shows that you are organised and have nothing to hide.

The initial contact is all about making the right impression so here is some advice:

DO	DON'T
Do write in the appropriate language when applying abroad if you can.	Don't presume that people from other countries speak English. This is often interpreted as arrogance on your part.
Do produce your letter on a word-processor if possible. If you handwrite it make sure it is clear and easily understood.	Do not write it on paper that has just been ripped out of a notepad or anything similar.
	Do not write it in any colour other than black or blue. Some

Suzanne Smith,
6 Oxford Street,
Northbridge,
Cumbria.
PN35 8YJ
29 February 2002

Monsieur Jean-Paul Chateau,
The Manager,
Belair Hotel,
Chamonix,
France.

Monsieur,

I am interested in the position of Bar Supervisor that you advertised in Skiing Today.

As you will see from the enclosed Curriculum Vitae, I am very experienced in hotel and bar work and I also speak French. I am keen to work in France as I enjoy the French culture and one of my passions is skiing which I would hope to do in my spare time.

I would be grateful if you would consider me for interview or advise me on the next stage of the application.

I look forward to hearing from you.

Yours faithfully,

Suzanne Smith

Suzanne Smith

Fig. 7. Sample letter to an individual or small company.

people will be greatly offended if it is written in red or green.

Do write it formally. Address the recipient Dear Sir, Dear Madam, Dear Mr or Dear Mrs.

Do not, even if the advertisement includes their Christian name, addressed them as Dear Tony or Dear Liz. This shows a lack of respect and the employer may presume that you could be disrespectful at work.

If you've addressed the recipient as 'Dear Mr Smith' you finish the letter with 'Yours sincerely'. If you started with a 'Dear Sir' you finish with 'Yours faithfully'.

Do not finish the letter with just 'Yours'.

Do print your name under your signature.

Do not just sign the letter. Your signature may look legible to you but it can be unreadable to someone else. The recipient might therefore not know who to address the reply to and consequently not bother. You lose any chance of an interview.

Do include all the information that the application form asks for.

Do not presume that there are some things that your prospective employer doesn't need to know. It may hinder your chances or make it appear that you are trying to hide something.

COMPOSING YOUR CV

A CV is simply a record of you, of your achievements, hobbies and work.

You will see from the example later in this chapter that it is normally written in reverse order starting with your most recent achievements and normally finishing at the date you started secondary education. If you have any difficulty in composing your CV you can obtain advice from your local school, college, careers company or jobseeker's club. A jobseeker's club is normally located at your local Jobcentre.

Getting the CV typed

If you don't own a typewriter or a word-processor contact your local school or college or the jobseeker's club as they might be able to help. They might also be able to give you photocopies to keep for reference. If this fails look in the local free paper for somebody advertising to produce CVs. It is better to pay a few pounds to them, and create the right impression, than lose the chance of a job. They will also make you multiple copies of your CV so that you have spares to use for other applications.

Compiling your CV

Take your time when compiling your CV. Prepare it thoroughly. Your success depends on it. Another applicant for the job may have inferior qualifications to you but appears to be better because of a superior CV.

Don't tell lies in your CV but experiment with ways of making a better impression. For example, look at the work experience of Jane in the sample CV in this chapter. Her first job was stacking shelves in a supermarket when they became low on stock. She could have called herself a shelf stacker but stock control assistant sounds much better.

Other points to observe are:

- Don't make your CV too long. Two or three sides of A4 paper is quite sufficient. If yours runs to more than this you must edit it. A prospective employer doesn't want to wade through page after page of waffle.

- Produce it on good quality paper. It gives the recipient the impression that you have made a special effort and that their job is important to you.

- It must be typewritten. You may think that your handwriting is legible but a well typed and composed CV is infinitely better.

- Don't send a photocopy of your CV. The quality of the paper will be poor. The print may also be grey rather than dark. The employer will get the impression that you have sent out scores of applications and his job is nothing special.

- Avoid technical jargon. The employer *may* not understand what you mean.

- Avoid slang. He *may* understand what you mean but will not be impressed.

Altering your CV

The example in Figure 8 is not the only way to construct a CV. You can alter the headings to suit your own qualifications and experience. However, most CVs generally follow this pattern.

If you do change this structure, try several different formats then get a relative or friend to look it over. It must look neat, professional and contain all of the vital information. It must also present you in the most favourable light possible.

Name:	Jane Jobseeker.
Address:	123 High Street, Workborough, Wessex. WE2 4UP
Tel:	01234 567890
Date of Birth:	29 February, 1980.
Nationality:	British.
Education:	1996–1998. Workborough Sixth Form College, Green Lane, Workborough. A Levels; English Language (B), Mathematics (C), French (C). 1991–1996. Wessex School, Early Road, Workborough. GCSEs: English Language (A), Mathematics (B), French (B), German (C), Science (C), Geography (C), History (C).
Work Experience:	Cutprice Supermarket, Sept 1996 to present date. Friday evenings and weekends. Started as Stock Control Assistant in 1996 and recently promoted to Cashier.
Interests:	Member of St John Ambulance Brigade. Competition standard at both basketball and horse-riding.
Other Information:	I hold current St John First Aid Certificate I hold provisional driving licence – taking test in three weeks time I am currently studying for the National Basketball Coaches Award.

Fig. 8. Sample CV.

FILLING IN THE APPLICATION FORM

Always complete the form in blue or black ink, unless it specifically states on the form that it should be typewritten. Always write in capital letters, again, unless specified differently. Read the application form thoroughly before starting to fill it in.

Sometimes in your excitement to apply for your dream job you are tempted to mail it as soon as possible. This often leads to things being missed off that you later realise would have been advantageous to include. Rushing it also leads to untidy writing. Both situations can be easily avoided.

First, take your time. One extra day isn't going to make much difference. Second, before you write anything on the form, write it on another sheet of paper and see if it looks right. Don't forget that the employer will get more applications than there are jobs available. So he has to eliminate some at the initial stage before drawing up a short-list for interview. Don't let yours be one of the discarded ones through lack of thought and preparation. Think of everything. It's essential that you do. Refer back to Chapter 1 if it helps. Double- check that you've included all your skills and qualities on the application.

A specimen application for the Mark Warner organisation is shown in Figure 9 and will give you an idea of what to expect.

SUPPLYING REFERENCES

This was covered in Chapters 1 and 6. Refer to those sections again if you need to. However, please remember that the terms 'reference' and 'testimonial' often get confused so please ascertain exactly what your employer requires.

OBTAINING AN INTERVIEW

It is quite normal if you don't receive a reply to your job application for quite some time. Don't worry about it. Remember that the employers will have received many replies and they want to read them all before compiling a short list for interview. What may seem like weeks of waiting to you is probably much less. It always seems longer when you are anxious, but don't waste this time.

Presume that you have been unsuccessful with this application and continue to look for other jobs. This not only makes the days go faster but it also prepares you for the worst. When the letter arrives, offering an interview, it becomes a great relief and cause for celebration.

Throughout the time leading up to the interview you should still be applying for other jobs, because:

(a) You might not be offered the job after the interview.
(b) You might attend the interview and find that the job was not what you expected it to be.
(c) You might discover another job that you prefer.

Mark Warner

Application Form

Return to:
Mark Warner
Personnel Department
George House
61-65 Kensington Church Street
London W8 4BA
Telephone: 0171-393 3178

Read carefully and complete in block capitals. Delete where necessary.

For office use only

Season applying for :   Winter / Summer

Position(s) applying for :   1 _____
(If more than one give
order of preference.)   2 _____

3 _____

LC		
LD		
ID		
IT		

Personal Particulars

Surname _____   Christian names _____

Present Address _____   Married / Single / Divorced / Engaged _____

_____   Age _____   Date of Birth _____

_____   Height _____

Telephone no. _____   Weight _____

Home Address _____   Nationality _____

_____   Type of passport _____

_____   Passport No. _____

Telephone no. _____   National Insurance No. _____

Next of Kin _____   Driving licence No. _____

Address _____   Date of issue _____

_____   Endorsements _____

_____   _____

Telephone no. _____

General education
Please give details of full time schooling commencing from age 11.

Dates From To	Name and Type of School	Examinations Taken + Grades Specify GCE, CSE or other

---

Fig. 9.   Sample application form.

Further education and training

Please give details of any studies/courses, academic or non academic, that you have undertaken since leaving school. State if full time, day release, evening or correspondence courses

Dates From To	Name of university college or school	Type of course	Subjects studied	Qualifications on leaving

Non academic achievements and spare time activities

Please include any certificates obtained and details of membership to teams, clubs and societies. Also mention how you spend your leisure time now.

_____

_____

_____

_____

_____

_____

_____

_____

_____

_____

_____

_____

_____

_____

_____

_____

_____

_____

_____

_____

Present employment

Name and address of employer

_____

Telephone no.

Position

Duties and responsibilities

Date of employment

How much notice you are required to give

May we contact this employer for a reference   Yes/No

Fig. 9. Cont.

103

Previous employment
List your previous positions leading up to your present position. Include relevant holiday and part time jobs and mark any employers that can be contacted for a reference with a *

Dates From To	Name and address of employer	Tel no.	Job title and brief description of responsibilities and duties

Skiing and water sports
Please complete the following sections.

How many weeks have you skied

In which resorts

How would you rate your skiing ability: (Please tick)

Strong fluent parallel skier on and off piste	☐
Strong fluent parallel skier on piste only	☐
Competent parallel skier	☐
Intermediate skier	☐
Stem Christie skier	☐
Beginner / Never skied	☐

Any other comments

How many years experience have you had

Sailing

Board sailing

Water skiing

How would you rate your ability in the following:

Dinghy sailing: Expert/Advanced/Intermediate / Beginner

Board sailing: Expert/Advanced/Intermediate / Beginner

Water skiing: Expert/Advanced/Intermediate / Beginner

In which of the above do you have a sound technical knowledge of equipment and equipment handling

Are you experienced in maintaining outboard engines   Yes/No

Do you have a boat drivers licence   Yes/No

If yes which one

Fig. 9. Cont.

General
All applicants should complete this section

*How did you hear of **Mark Warner***

Have you applied to us before   Yes/no.   If yes, when   *For what position*

Are you willing to work in any of our resorts

When will you be available? From   *Until*

Do you know of any other person applying with whom you would like to work, if Yes give name

Do you have any physical disabilities   Yes/no   If yes, what are they

Do you have any problems with your health e.g. Asthma, Diabetes

Do you speak any of the following foreign languages (Please tick)

	No	Basic	Conversational	Good Standard	Fluent
French	☐	☐	☐	☐	☐
German	☐	☐	☐	☐	☐
Italian	☐	☐	☐	☐	☐
Greek	☐	☐	☐	☐	☐
Turkish	☐	☐	☐	☐	☐

*Describe briefly why you wish to work for **Mark Warner***

What do you expect the position you have applied for to involve

Why do you feel you would be particularly suitable for this position

Declaration

The facts set forth in this application are, to the best of my knowledge, true and complete:

Signature   **Date**

Fig. 9. Cont.

Preparing for the interview

Once you are given an interview, don't just sit back with a warm glow and presume that you have the job. There will be several other interviewees and the person who succeeds will be the one who is most impressive at the interview. The difference is *preparation*.

First, and this is most important, note the time, date and place of the interview in your diary or somewhere where you cannot lose it or forget it.

Second, if it gives the name of the interviewer, make sure you know what sex they are and how to pronounce their name. If you are unsure about any of this you should telephone their personal secretary and check on the facts. Don't be embarrassed. You will not be regarded as someone who is unsure or lacking in confidence. You will actually give the impression of somebody who is organised and likes to be thoroughly prepared.

Then, out of courtesy, write to thank them for offering you an interview and confirm the time and date that you will be attending.

Research counts

Now the work begins that can mean the difference between success and failure.

If you have applied to a company the chances are that they will have sent you some literature about their operation. Read it thoroughly. Make notes about the things you consider are big advantages in the job and also anything that you want to ask questions about. During the interview you will have the opportunity to use this information.

If you are seeking to work for a smaller firm who doesn't give out this sort of literature they will be more difficult to research. Nevertheless, you should still try to find out as much about them as is possible and the local reference library is a good place to start. They should carry details of all small limited companies and all back issues of numerous newspapers including the regional daily. You can also use the technique that was suggested in the earlier chapters regarding finding a job – that of talking to local people. This could be at the library, the local pub, newsagents, garage, anywhere.

The above techniques can be used if applying to a sports club but you could also do the following:

(a) You should be able to find out performance details and other background information about the club in your sport's specialist magazine or local newspaper.

(b) You should quite easily find people who have played or worked for this club and talk to them. There should also be plenty of players who have competed against them to give you an alternative opinion.

Making notes

Don't try to remember everything that you find out but make notes about it. You may think that you will only find out a small amount of information which will be easily remembered and this might be true. However, if you find out more than you anticipated, some of the earlier data may be forgotten, so write it down. This will also be useful to revise from later in the process and could be helpful for formulating questions to ask in the interview.

ATTENDING THE INTERVIEW OR A SPORTS TRIAL

There are certain things that are of the utmost importance when attending an interview. Ignore them at your peril.

- Don't be late.

- Don't turn up on the wrong day.

- Note the location of the interview.

If you are unsure how to get there check in an A to Z guide of the area, if one exists, or check on an Ordnance Survey map. If still unsure, enquire about directions with the secretary. This could be discussed in your initial contact with her or it could be included with your interview invitation. It is also a good idea to ask her about car parking. Many a candidate has been late for an interview even though they had arrived in plenty of time, because they couldn't find a parking spot. There is also the possibility of getting stuck in a one-way system or roadworks, so ask about these as well and allow plenty of time.

These enquiries show excellent interview preparation and the secretary is bound to mention this to her boss.

Succeeding in the interview

When you eventually get into the interview a few essential points are worth observing:

1. Be smartly dressed. If you can't make the effort to look good it will be taken as a sign that you will not make the effort in the job and could produce shoddy work.

2. Be polite. Even if the interviewer introduces himself as Bill Jones, still call him Mr Jones throughout the interview.

3. Address the interviewer(s) by name. If he hasn't introduced himself, it is a big plus point for you to say 'Good Morning, you must be Mr Jones.'

4. Look interested and confident. When the interviewer talks to you or you are replying, look them straight in the eye. If you are nervous and look at the floor or out of the window, this may be taken as a sign of disinterest or that you lack the confidence that they require.

Asking questions

Details of an excellent book *How to Win at Job Hunting* are given in the Further Reading section. This book goes into great detail about the sort of questions you could ask and those that may be asked of you.

Asking questions at the end of an interview shows that you are still interested in the job – but don't overdo it. Remember the interviewer(s) might be on a tight schedule. Only one or two questions are recommended.

A big mistake is to ask questions that have been covered in their literature or during the interview. Interviewers will get the impression that you have been inattentive. If there is something from either that you didn't understand, you can get away with these questions by asking 'there was one thing that I was unsure of from the brochure (or from the interview)'. In this way you have already acknowledged that you know that it has already been covered.

Good questions to ask would be about:

- Training – especially if this is your first job.

- Colleagues – who your superiors and subordinates would be.

- Salary – not recommended early in the interview as this appears to be all that you are interested in. At the end, though, it is vital that you ask about this if you haven't been told.

- Responsibilities – what are you responsible for, and are there any foreseeable problems?

SUMMARY

- Take your time with your application letter – make it neat and formal.

- Fill in the application form in blue or black ink – neatly.

- Take your time with your CV – type it and don't omit anything.

- Keep all of your references and testimonials neat and tidy – they are very valuable.

- When offered an interview still apply for other jobs.

- Be early for your interview – dress smartly and be polite.

- Revise for your interview – make a note of the questions you want to ask.

8

Accepting the Offer and Making Other Arrangements

ACCEPTING THE OFFER

If things have gone to plan, you are reading this section after you have been offered employment. Now you will need to tidy up some loose ends. But first, accept the offer.

The letter of acceptance (see Figure 10) is a simple confirmation and a gesture of thanks but you may also want to ask some questions that have not been covered by the employer. Things like terms of employment should have been given to you by now but, if they haven't, you can enquire about them in your acceptance letter.

The terms of employment

These should include a job description, salary, weekly hours, holiday arrangements, any training necessary for the job, overtime pay and other relevant arrangements. If you are working abroad the arrangements for National Insurance contributions (see later section in this chapter) should also be addressed.

If any of this has not been given to you in writing you should ask for it in your letter. If your job is abroad, you should ask your employer whether they take care of any visa arrangements, or if it is your responsibility.

TRAINING FOR THE JOB

If you have accepted employment from private individuals or by a small company, then it is very likely that they will expect you to have already trained for this job. You should already have the experience or qualifications necessary to conduct all the required tasks of this work. Refer back to Chapter 6 if necessary.

Alternatively, if you are due to work for a big company then the majority of them conduct their own training courses so that, even if you are already qualified, you are inducted into their way of doing things. This training period is a good time to meet your new

Suzanne Smith,
6 Oxford Street,
Northbridge,
Cumbria.
PN35 8YJ
Tel: 01987 654321
29 February 1999

Monsieur Jean-Paul Chateau,
The Manager,
Belair Hotel,
Chamonix,
France.

Monsieur,
   Thank you for offering me the position of Bar Supervisor at your hotel. I am very pleased to accept the position and I'm looking forward to working with you in such a beautiful part of France.
   One thing, however, that we didn't discuss in the interview was my National Insurance contributions and I would be pleased if you could inform me of the arrangements for these.

Yours faithfully,

Suzanne Smith

Suzanne Smith

Fig. 10. Sample letter accepting employment.

employers, superiors and colleagues and also gives you a chance to get mistakes out of the way before it could prove to be expensive.
   If you have been offered a job that doesn't give training and you are not confident enough to go straight into it, or maybe you are qualified but have had a long break from this type of work, then it may be a good idea to look for relevant voluntary work before starting with your new employer.

OBTAINING A PASSPORT

If you are British and working in Britain you can skip this section. If you plan to work abroad you will need some or all of the following documents before you can work legally in a foreign country.

Obtaining a passport for a British Citizen is fairly straightforward as long as you apply in plenty of time. The Passport Office recommend that you apply at least one month in advance. It is possible to get a passport quicker than this but it will involve you in a long journey to your designated passport office, an extra £10 fee and entail waiting in a queue before being attended to.

Passport enquiries can be made on (0990) 210410. Offices are located at:

BELFAST.
Hampton House,
47–53 High Street,
Belfast, BT1 2QS.
Tel. (01232) 232371

GLASGOW.
3 Northgate,
96 Milton Street,
Cowcaddens,
Glasgow, G4 0BT.
Tel. (0141) 332 0271

LONDON.
(only urgent personal applications)
Clive House,
70 Petty France,
London SW1 9HD
Tel. (0171) 279 3434

LIVERPOOL.
5th Floor,
India Buildings,
Water Street,
Liverpool, L2 0QZ.
Tel. (0151) 237 3010

NEWPORT.
Olympia House,
Upper Dock Street,
Newport, NP9 1XA
Tel. (01633) 244500

PETERBOROUGH.
Aragon Court,
Northminster Road,
Peterborough, PE1 1QC.
Tel. (01733) 895555

Application forms can be obtained at main Post Offices and many travel agents. You will need two small photographs of yourself and one of them must be countersigned by a referee (someone like a doctor, teacher or clergyman).

Always keep your passport safe and make a note of its number and place of issue in case of difficulties or, more particularly, if it is stolen or you lose it. It is also a good idea to leave a photocopy of its main page at home before departure.

OBTAINING VISAS AND WORK PERMITS

If your employment is in the European Union there is no need to obtain a visa or work permit before starting work. For many other countries outside the EU you will need both to be able to work there. Obtaining these can be a very lengthy and difficult process so start negotiating this as soon as possible after being offered the job.

If you are lucky, as mentioned earlier in this chapter, your employer may take care of this for you. However, if you are not, you need to contact the consular section of the appropriate embassy as soon as possible. These are generally found in London and are quite easy to trace through *Yellow Pages* or your local library. The consul will then advise you of the procedure which normally requires you to supply the following:

- Your passport
- Your birth certificate
- A medical certificate
- Your educational qualifications (see Chapter 6)
- Two passport size photographs
- Your marriage certificate (if this is relevant).

TAKING MEDICAL PRECAUTIONS

If you are taking up a job in Britain you can miss this section but a few of the points below should be noted, especially if you are going to work in remote areas overseas.

Over recent years the health care in many countries has become as good as that in Britain but it can be costly to obtain it. Not many have a 'free' health service like ours so a few precautions are well worth taking before taking up employment abroad.

1. First, make sure you are fit for the job. If it is going to be strenuous, work out before you go. Also ensure you are medically fit.

2. Have all your check-ups before you go – dental, medical and optical.

3. If you wear glasses take a spare pair. If you use any other appliances, and a spare set is out of the question, make sure you have the appliance serviced. In the case of battery-driven aids, such as for hearing, make sure you take a spare battery.

4. Have a course of vaccinations. These can take some time so check with your GP early. Typhoid for example requires two injections, each being one month apart. You can normally find out from the

embassy which vaccinations are required but the Department of Health also produces a leaflet on this. Enquire at your local surgery.

5. Take with you any medication that you would normally use in Britain. If on an extended visit make sure you have enough to cover its duration. Also take a first aid box that might include, as well as the usual plasters, antiseptic cream and paracetamol, things like:

- Insect repellant
- Anti-malaria pills
- Travel sickness tablets
- Anti-diarrhoea medication

and don't forget you may probably need suntan lotion!

6. If you are working in the EEC obtain Form E111 from the Post Office. This will provide you with emergency medical service while you are abroad. It must be stressed that this is emergency treatment only. If you need to stay in hospital after the initial treatment you will have to pay for it so it is well worth taking out insurance (this will normally be an all-in policy which also covers you for loss of equipment, baggage, money, passports, etc.).

It must also be noted that you may have to pay for this emergency treatment whilst abroad and reclaim the costs when you return to Britain. In most cases you will not be able to reclaim the full amount but you might be able to reclaim the difference through your insurers. Check before taking out the policy.

COMPLYING WITH NATIONAL INSURANCE REQUIREMENTS

You need to know, before you leave, what the arrangements are for your National Insurance contributions. Your new employer should be able to tell you this. If they are not sure, however, you can obtain advice and information from your local Social Security office or, if working abroad, from the Overseas Branch of the Department of Social Security, Newcastle upon Tyne, NE98 1YX.

You need this cover in case you lose your job, fall ill or need to claim benefits whether abroad or in Britain.

TRAVELLING THERE

If you're working in the UK you should be able to plan your travelling arrangements by discussing them with family and friends or by contacting your local bus, train or flight operator.

If you are working abroad you might need to make special arrangements but usually your employer will help to take care of everything for you and the cost is normally included as part of your contract.

If you do have to make your own arrangements, however, there are a few points to remember:

1. Make your arrangements early. If you leave it late you might not be able to find discounted travel or, indeed, you might not be able to get there at all.

2. Look for the most convenient and suitable way of getting to your destination – the cheapest is not always best.

3. Arrange travel insurance that covers you for cancellations, delays, loss of luggage, etc. Take advice from a travel agent or insurance broker if it helps.

SUMMARY

- Write a letter of acceptance. Use it as a chance to enquire about matters you are not clear about – especially the terms of employment.

- Train or prepare yourself for the job.

- Make early arrangements for passports, visas and work permits.

- Take out insurance. Make sure it covers everything.

- Ensure you are physically fit – get medical, dental and optical check-ups.

- Take a first aid case.

- Make travel arrangements early.

Useful Addresses

COMPANY REFERENCES (CO)

Airtours Plc
: Personnel Dept, Wavell House, Holcombe Road,
Helmshore, Lancashire BB4 4NB
Tel. (01706) 909027 (24 hours)

Backroads
: 801 Cedar Street, Berkley,
California 94710-1800, USA.
Tel. 800 462 2848

BUNAC
: Bunacamp Counsellors, 16 Bowling Green Lane, London EC1R 0BD.
Tel. (0171) 251 3472

Camp America
: Applications Office, American Institute for ForeignStudy, 37A Queens Gate, London SW7 5HR.
Tel. (0171) 581 7377

Canvas Holidays
: Overseas Personnel Dept, 12 Abbey Park Place, Dunfermline KY12 7PD.
Tel. (01383) 644018

Crystal Holidays
: Arlington Rd, Surbiton, Surrey
KT6 6BW.

Eurocamp Plc
: Overseas Recruitment Dept, Canute Court, Toft Road, Knutsford, Chesire WA16 0NL.
Tel. (01565) 625522

European Waterways
: 35 Wharf Road, Wraysbury, Staines, Middlesex TW19 5JQ.
Tel. (01784) 482439

Halsbury Travel Ltd
: 35 Churchill Park, Colwick Business Estate, Nottingham NG4 2HF.
Tel. (07000) 150300

Keycamp
: Overseas Recruitment Dept, 92–96 Lind Road, Sutton, Surrey SM1 4PL.
Tel. (0181) 395 8201

Mark Warner
Resorts Personnel Dept, Prefer you to telephone.
Tel. (0171) 393 3178

PGL Young Adventure
Alton Court, Penyard Lane (874), Ross on Wye HR9 5NR.
Tel. (01989) 767833

BOOK REFERENCES (BK)

Summer Jobs Abroad
Ed. David Woodworth. Vacation Work Pubs. Contains information on employment at: Belle France, Bombard Balloon Adventures (USA), Club Mediteranee, Colossus Beach Hotel (Greece), Emperor Divers (Egypt), Errislannan Manor (Ireland), Rotfluhhotel (Austria), Tennis Club Zinal (Switzerland), West of Ireland Activity Centre.

MAGAZINE REFERENCES (MAG)

Cycling Plus
Future Publishing Ltd., Somerton, Somerset.
Tel. (01225) 822511
For details on French Country Camping (Cycle Maintenance and Assembly.)

Golf Weekly
EMAP Publishing Ltd, Bretton, Peterborough PE3 8DZ.
Tel. (01733) 264666
For details on Came Down Golf Club, Drayton Park Golf Club, Hever Golf Club, Jack Nicklaus Golf Centre, Lamberhurst Golf Club, The London Golf Club, Royal Ashdown Forest Golf Club, Tandridge Golf Club, Three Rivers Golf Club, (all Britain) and Golf Centrum, Rotterdam and La Moye Golf Club Jersey.

Rugby World
IPC Magazines, Kings Reach Tower, Stamford St, London SE1 9LS.
Tel. (0171) 261 6830
For details on Muscat Rugby Club, S.A.F. and Brussels British Rugby Club.

NEWSPAPER REFERENCES (NEWS)

Jobsearch
50–56 Portman Road, Reading, Berks RG30 1BA
Tel. (0118) 9490600

Overseas Jobs Express	Premier House, Shoreham Airport, West Sussex BN43 5FF. Tel. (01273) 440220 or 440540 For details on Ski Esprit, Village Camps Skiing and Voluntary Service Overseas.
The Stage	47 Bermondsey Street, London SE1 3XT Fax. (0171) 357 9287 For details on cruise ships, singers, pianists, comedians, etc.

INTERNET REFERENCES (INT)

LYCOS engine, subheading Coolworks for:
NATIONAL PARKS – Grand Canyon, Death Valley, Everglades, Mount Rushmore and Yellowstone.

USA SKI RESORTS – Alpine Meadows, Alta Ski, Aspen, Badger Pass, Bear Mountain, Big Sky, Boreal, Breckenridge, Copper Mountain, Cowboy Village, Crested Butte, Crystal Mountain, Diamond Peak, Eldorada, Flagg Ranch, Heavenly, Hidden Valley, Hunter Mountain, Keystone, Lone Mountain, Loon Mountain, Mammoth Mountain, Mission Ridge, Mount Bachelor, Mount Snow, Northstar, Okemo, Purgatory, Roaring Fork, Royal Gorge Cross, Shanty Creek, Snowbasin, Snowbird, Soda Springs, Sonnenalp, Steamboat, Stratton Mountain, Sugarbush, Sunday River, Taos, Telluride, Timberline, Vail, Waterville Valley, Winter Park, Woodspur Lodge.

Camp Duncan, Illinois, USA.

INFOSEEK engine, subheading Summer Jobs for:
Hooligan Ranch, New Mexico, USA.
Lazy-H Ranch, Wyoming, USA.
Lazy-L&B Ranch, Wyoming, USA.
Lit'le Mary Ranch, New Mexico, USA.

INFOSEEK engine, subheading Sports Jobs for:
Angel Fire Resort, New Mexico, USA.
Camden County YMCA, New Jersey, USA.
City of Virginia Beach, Virginia, USA.
Global Apparel, USA (multinational).
Human Resources & Kinetics, Illinois, USA.
Just Cruising International, Caribbean.
Sports Equipment International, Indiana, USA.
Tampa Bay Mutiny, Florida, USA.
United States Tennis Association, White Plains, New York, USA.
Western Professional Hockey League, Phoenix, USA.
West Michigan Whitecaps, USA.

INFOSEEK engine, subheading Coolworks for:
Aspen Lodge and Estes Park, Colorado, USA.
B-Bar Guest Ranch, Montana, USA.
Clear Creek Ranch, North Carolina, USA.
Cowboy Village, Wyoming, USA.
Drowsy Water Ranch, Colorado, USA.
Great Alaska Fish Camp, Alaska, USA.
Home Ranch, Colorado, USA.
Kiawah Island Resort, Carolina, USA.
Lake Powell Resort, Carolina, USA.
Lone Mount Ranch, Montana, USA.
Lost Creek Ranch, Wyoming, USA.
Sea Pines Resort, South Carolina, USA.
Vista Verde Ranch, Colorado, USA.

YAHOO engine, subheading Employment for:
Cleminson University, South Carolina, USA.
Cleveland State University, USA.
Dubuquee University, Iowa, USA.
Georgia Games, Marietta, USA.
Hilton Heat, South Carolina, USA.
La Cross Bobcats, Wisconsin, USA.
Professional Cycling League, USA.
Tampa Bay Rowdies, Florida, USA.
Thomas Jefferson High School, Virginia, USA.
United States Squash Racquets Association, Philadelphia, USA.
United States Tennis Association, Flushing Meadows, New York, USA.
University of Maine, USA.
University of North Carolina, USA.
University of Kansas, USA.
University of Southern California, USA.
University of Hawaii, USA.
West Michigan Whitecaps, USA.

EQUESTRIAN TIMES Internet address:
http://www.horsenews.com/classified/job-vacant.htm for:
Arundel Farm, New Zealand.
High Meadow Ranch, California, USA.

Further Reading

PUBLICATIONS RECOMMENDED WITHIN THE TEXT

A Guide to Jobs and Qualifications in Sport and Recreation, John Potter/ILAM (John Potter Publications).

A Guide to Professional Sport, Various (The Institute of Professional Sport).

Careers in Sport, Compendium (The Sports Council).

Getting a Job Abroad, Roger Jones (How To Books).

Getting a Job in Travel and Tourism, Mark Hempshell (How To Books).

How To Find Temporary Work Abroad, Nick Vandome (How To Books).

How To Travel Round the World, Nick Vandome (How To Books).

How To Win at Job Hunting, Ian Maitland (Century Business).

Playing at the Top: A Guide To Professional Sport, Various (Institute of Professional Sport).

Sports Scholarships and College Programs in the USA, ed. Ron Walker (Petersons).

Summer Jobs Abroad, ed. David Woodworth (Vacation Work Publications).

The International Directory of Voluntary Work, ed. David Woodworth (Vacation Work Publications).

The Voluntary Agencies Directory, Various (NCVO Publications).

Volunteer Work, (The Central Bureau for Educational Visits & Exchanges).

SUGGESTED FURTHER READING

Most of the books listed below are available from the 'Job' section of your public library but if you run into difficulties it should be possible to order them from major book stores by quoting the details provided.

A Year off ... or a Year On, Suzanne Straw (Hobson/CRAC)

Careers in Sport, Louise Fyfe (Kogan Page)

Careers in Sport Compendium, Louise Fyfe (Kogan Page)

Careers in Teaching, Ewan McLeish (Trotman)

Careers in the Travel Industry, C. Chester (Kogan Page)

Cruise Ship Job Guide, John Kenning (Harp Publications)

Cruise Ship Job Guide, John Kenning (Harp Publications)
Live & Work in France/Germany/Italy/Spain & Portugal, (Vacation Work Pubs.)
Summer Jobs USA, Petersons Guides (Vacation Work Pubs.)
Taking a Year Off, Val Butcher (Trotman)
Working Abroad, Susan Griffith (Kogan Page)
Working in Ski Resorts, V. Pybus & C. James (Vacation Work Pubs.)
Working in Leisure, COIC (COIC)

MAGAZINES & NEWSPAPERS

Anglers Mail, IPC Magazines, Kings Reach Tower, Stamford Street, London SE1 9LS.
Angling Times, EMAP Publishing, Bretton Court, Peterborough PE3 8DZ.
Athletics Weekly, EMAP Publishing Ltd, Bretton Peterborough PE3 8DZ.
Boat International, 5 Kingston Hill, Kingston on Thames, Surrey KT2 7PW.
Sports Boat & Waterski International, Brinkworth House, Chippenham SN15 5DF.
British Horse, British Horse Society, Stoneleigh, Kennilworth CV8 2LR.
Camping Magazine, Link House, Dingwall Avenue, Croydon CR9 2TA.
Cycling Plus, Future Publishing, 30 Monmouth Street, Bath BA1 2BW.
Cycling World, Andrew House, 2a Granville Road, Sidcup, Kent DA14 4BN.
Mountain Biker International, United Leisure Magazines, PO Box 3205, 4 Selsdon Way, London E14 9GL.
Footballers World, Newton Wells, 57 High Street, Hampton, Middlesex TW12 2SX.
World Soccer, IPC Magazines, Kings Reach Tower, Stamford Street, London SE1 9LS.
Golf Monthly, IPC Magazines, Kings Reach Tower, Stamford Street, London SE1 9LS.
The Golfer, Village Green Publishing, 24a Brook Mews N, Paddington, London W2 3BW.
Golf Weekly, EMAP Publishing Ltd., Bretton Court, Bretton, Peterborough PE3 8DZ. Tel. (01733) 264666
Hockey Digest, Unit E6, Aladdin Workspace, 426 Long Drive, Greenford, Middlesex UB6 8UH.
Martial Arts Today, HLL Publications Ltd., Greater London House, Hampstead, London NW1 7QQ.
Rugby World, IPC Magazines, Kings Reach Tower, Stamford St., London SE1 9LS.

The Good Ski Guide, 91 High Street, Esher, Surrey KT10 9QD.

Sport Diver, Market Link Publishing, Tye Green, Elsenham, Bishops Stortford CM22 6DY.

Sports Quarterly, The Vinegar Factory, 20 Bowden Street, London SE11 4DS.

Swimming Times, Harold Fern House, Derby Square, Loughborough LE11 0AL.

Tennis Ace, The LTA, Queens Club, London W14 9EG.

Tennis World, The Spendlove Centre, Enstone Road, Charlbury, Oxon OX7 3PQ.

Total Fitness Magazine, 260 Great North Road, Woodlands, Doncaster DN6 7HP.

Windsurf, The Blue Barn, Thew Lane, Wootton, Woodstock, Oxon OX7 1HA.

Yachting Monthly, IPC Magazines, Kings Reach Tower, Stamford Street, London SE1 9LS.

Yachting World, IPC Magazines, Kings Reach Tower, Stamford Street, London SE1 9LS.

Yachts & Yachting, 196 Eastern Esplanade, Southend, Sussex SS1 3AB.

FOR WORK NOT DIRECTLY CONNECTED TO YOUR SPORT

There are also many overseas opportunities advertised in the following journals that are available from most leading newsagents or through your local reference library.

Entertainment – *Melody Maker, Record Mirror, The Stage, The White Book*.

General – *Overseas Jobs Express, Job Search*.

Nannies, Servants, Chalet Maids etc. – *The Lady, Nursing Times*.

Careers Europe is a centre set up to access information regarding work in Europe. It cannot be approached directly, so first you have to contact a Jobcentre who will phone them and obtain the advice and information that you need. Amongst their services they produce a wide range of Eurofact sheets covering different aspects of working, training and studying in the European Community.

Glossary

Abseiling. A rock-climbing term for descending down a rock-face, or any other near vertical structure, using only a rope and possibly a harness. The Royal Marines and SAS are often seen on TV doing this at great speed.

Accessing. A term used in computing to denote entering a computer programme; a term used commonly for the Internet.

Activity Holidays. Holidays during which the holidaymakers take part in one or more activities such as golf, tennis or windsurfing.

Assistantship. See Graduate Assistantship.

BMX. The full title is Bicycle Moto Cross. Participants race against each other on specially adapted bikes over rough terrain.

BTEC. The abbreviation of Business and Technician Education Council. A body that administers many sports-related courses and examinations. See Chapter 6.

BUNAC. The abbreviation of the British Universities North America Club. They have been arranging employment at summer camps in the USA and Canada since 1962. They now also arrange work in other countries like Australia, Ghana, Jamaica, Malta, New Zealand, Spain and South Africa, but the latter is generally of the non-sporting type.

BUSA. The abbreviation of the British Universities Sports Association. A body that administers student sport in Britain and can also advise on scholarships.

Bursary. See also scholarships. Bursaries tend to be small grants to students whereas scholarships are much bigger and can be awarded to cover a longer period of time.

Camp Counselling. A job mainly in summer camps that entails looking after the needs of the younger participants on the course.

CCPR. The abbreviation of the Central Council for Physical Recreation. One of the oldest established sporting bodies in Britain.

City and Guilds. Short for the City and Guilds of London Institute. A body that administers many sports-related courses and examinations.

Curriculum Vitae. Normally abbreviated to CV. Literal meaning is 'history of life' but nowadays is simply a record of your education, employment and interests. Always asked for by prospective employers prior to drawing up a short list for interview.

Cyber Café. A commercial enterprise found on the high streets of many major cities that offers clients, for a fee, access to the internet. See also Internet Café.

Dude Ranches. A thriving, vibrant holiday retreat in North America that gives their guests a feel for the old Wild West (without too much discomfort).

Embassy. In the UK most embassies are normally found in London and are the British headquarters of friendly overseas countries. You need to contact them to arrange visas and work permits.

Graduate. A person who holds a degree from a university or college.

Graduate Assistantship. Normally abbreviated to Assistantship. These are places given to graduates. They normally receive a grant to cover the cost of their studies for a higher-level degree in return for some teaching or coaching. Sports Assistantships are usually found in the USA.

GNVQ. See also NVQ. Abbreviation of the General National Vocational Qualification. This is awarded by many colleges around Britain and many of their courses are sport based. More details in Chapter 6.

ILAM. An abbreviation of the Institute of Leisure and Amenity Management who administer their own internal examinations. See Chapter 6.

Internet. The Internet was developed in 1969 as a means of passing information from one computer to another. It has been referred to as 'the information superhighway' and it is a very fast way of accessing all kinds of information from around the world.

Internet Café. A commercial enterprise found on the high streets of many major cities that offer clients, for a fee, access to the Internet. See also Cyber Café.

Leisure Company. One of the growing number of companies set up to cater for holidaymakers' needs. They normally arrange things from flights, accommodation, and currency to sports courses.

NVQ. See also GNVQ. Abbreviation of National Vocational Qualification. This is awarded by many colleges around Britain and many of their courses are sport based. More details in Chapter 6.

Passport. A formal document issues by the Passport Office (see Chapter 8) that entitles you to leave Britain for another country. There are six Passport Offices around Britain.

Prize Money. Money gained by winning or being placed in a tournament. A precarious way of earning a living. If you don't win you don't eat!

Professional. In sporting terms, a person who makes a living out of sport.

Professional (Golf). A golf pro' makes a living out of coaching, organising tournaments and running the golf shop.

Professional (Tournament). A golf tournament pro' plays for a living and makes money out of being placed highly in tournaments as well as receiving sponsorship and advertising revenue.

PTI. Abbreviation of Physical Training Instructor. A position held in the Armed Forces. See Chapter 2.

References. A record of your employment with an employer who normally sends them, confidentially, on request to a prospective employer.

Representative. Normally abbreviated to Rep. These are usually people who represent a holiday company or similar organisation and are employed to look after clients.

Semi-Pro. A person who makes money through sport but not enough to live on so therefore has another job to boost his earnings.

Scholarship. Scholarships are grants that are often awarded to students that universities and colleges are keen to enrol. They vary in size from a couple of hundred pounds to thousands. See Chapter 2 for more details.

SCOTVEC. Abbreviation of Scottish Vocational Education Council who administer the equivalent of the BTEC qualification in Scotland. See Chapter 6.

Short list. A list of candidates for a job that has been reduced from all the applications. These are normally the ones that have been selected for interview.

Sponsorship. Funding given to sports people, mainly by commercial organisations, in return for the promotion of their product.

Sports Council. The Sports Council provides information on local authorities, governing bodies of sport and sports facilities. It has six regional offices. See Chapter 5 for the address of its HQ.

Summer Camps. Originally an American concept but now growing in popularity around the world. These holiday camps are set up to usefully occupy schoolchildren during their long summer break. Courses range from arts and crafts to numerous sports.

Terms of employment. A document that should be provided by an employer detailing the working practice and conditions of new employees.

Visa. Many countries outside of the EU require visitors to obtain an entry permit, or visa, from their embassy before being allowed through immigration.

VSO. An abbreviation of Voluntary Services Overseas. A long-established, reputable aid agency. See Chapter 3 for details.

Voluntary Work. Historically this was unpaid work for a charitable organisation. Now some of this work carries a salary. See Chapter 3 for details.

Work Permit. Many countries, outside the EU, require working visitors to obtain a work permit from their embassy before being allowed through immigration.

Year Out. Taking a year out is the term commonly used by students taking a break before either going to university or between college and their chosen career. Sometimes called a Gap Year.

INDEX